Manchester City
– Moments to Remember –

John Creighton

Wilmslow, England

Copyright ©, John Creighton, 1992, 1993

All Rights Reserved

No part of this publication may be reproduced, stored in a retrieval system, or transmitted in any form or by any means – electronic, mechanical, photocopying, recording, or otherwise – without prior written permission from the publisher.

First edition published in 1992; this new edition published in 1993
both by Sigma Leisure –
an imprint of Sigma Press, 1 South Oak Lane, Wilmslow, Cheshire, SK9 6AR

Whilst every effort has been made to ensure that the information given in this book is correct, neither the publisher nor the author accept any responsibility for any inaccuracy.

British Library Cataloguing in Publication Data
A CIP record for this book is available from the British Library.

Second edition ISBN: 1-85058-397-8

Cover designed by: Design House, Marple Bridge

Typesetting, page design and graphics by: Sigma Press

Printed and bound by: Manchester Free Press

Cover: David White has just scored in the October 1990 game with Manchester Utd

Acknowledgements

The Author and Publisher would like to thank a number of people, organisations and newspapers.

Particular thanks are extended to Manchester City Football Club for their co-operation in this venture. We thank them for permission to use the club crest, and also for the information and photographs provided.

We also gratefully acknowledge the help of the Football League and the Football Association, both of whom gave permission to use various statistics and tables. The Football League kindly put their records and archives at our disposal.

Every effort has been made to contact those who own original photographs, and the following have been most helpful in providing illustrations:

Whitbread p.l.c.; Evening Sentinel; Evening Gazette; Bolton Evening News; Illustrated London News; Evening Leader; Nottingham Evening Post; Documentary Photography Archive; Mr. Delves; Mr. Miles; Mrs. Kitchen; Mr. Gamble; Mr. Robinson; Mr. J. Heale; Mr. Montgomery; the Barkas family; Mike Dean.

Finally, our thanks go to City's Phil Critchley, and to Chairman, Peter Swales, for allowing the club's story to be told. However, the club is not responsible for any statistical or historical errors or omissions.

– Contents –

1. The Beginning	**1**
The Religious Influence	1
A New Name	1
Newton Heath Rivalry	2
Ardwick F.C. and Professional Football	2
The Alliance and the Football League	3
"Manchester City" and Meredith	4
Test Matches	5
New Players, Mixed Results	6
Division Two Champions, 1899	6
Into the First Division	7
2. The Early 1900s	**9**
Division Two Soccer	9
City – United Rivalry 1906-8	12
Relegation and Recovery	15
Manager Mangnall	18
The First World War	19
The Fire	21
Maine Road Move	23
The FA Cup and Meredith's return	24
Departures and Arrivals, 1924/25	27
Relegation	29
City -v- United, 1925/26	29
The Road to Wembley: 1926	30
Tommy Johnson and Matt Busby	33

3. The 1930s and 1940s	**35**
FA Cup Success 1932-34	35
Swift and Barkas	40
League Champions, 1937	42
The Second World War	44
Back to Division One, 1947	48
4. The 1950s	**51**
Manager McDowall	51
Bert Trautmann	54
Meadows, Revie and Leivers	54
Blues -v- Reds 1953/56	57
The FA Cup Final 1955	60
Wembley Again!	61
1957 FA Cup	64
5. The 1960s	**67**
League Upsets 1960-64	67
The League Cup and FA Cup 1960-65	67
Law, Young, Pardoe and Oakes	68
Mercer and Allison	70
Heslop, Summerbee, Bell and Book	71
Round Six of 1967 F.A. Cup	73
Reds and Blues go for the League	73
Francis Lee	75
European Soccer	77

6. The 1970s — 79
Manchester Clubs in Cup Games — 79
Into Europe — 80
The FA Cup, 1971 — 82
New Players — 83
Marsh and Davies — 83
Mercer and Allison Leave — 84
Three Managers in One Season — 86
Lee Goes, Law Returns — 86
Dennis Tueart — 87
League and the F.A. Cup 1973/74 — 88
1976 League Cup Final — 90
The League 1975/76 — 90
European Soccer in the late 1970s — 92
Arrivals & Departures 1977-79 — 94

7. 1980 – 1990 — 95
Bond To The Rescue? — 95
The FA Cup Competition 1981 — 96
The League Cup and the League — 97
Division One Soccer 1985/86 — 100
The FA Cup and the Littlewoods Cup — 102
New Signing – Andy Dibble — 104
Division One Again — 104
Banana Mania — 107
Division One Once More — 110
Littlewoods Cup — 113
New Signings — 114

8. The Early Nineties — 117
Early Success — 117
Qualifying for Europe — 120
1990/91 Cup Competitions — 128
The 1991/92 Season — 129
February '92: Championship Challenge carries on — 143
In the Top Three — 143
Easter Games, 1992 — 147
1991/92 Cup Competitions — 149
F.A. Cup 1991/92 — 149
The 1992/93 Season — 153
Premier League Soccer — 153
The New Stand Opens — 163
1992/93 Cup Competitions — 166
F.A. Cup 1992/93 — 167

Honours gained by Manchester City — 169

iv

1

The Beginning

The Religious Influence

Although Manchester City Football Club was designated a limited company in 1894, its origins go back to 1880.

The idea of a club was hatched in the parish of St Mark's, West Gorton, Manchester, and much of the initial work can be attributed to the vicar's daughter. She suggested to Reverend Arthur Connell that he might establish a Workingmen's Club. This led to the formation of a cricket team in 1879, and a football club the following year.

The working class area of Gorton provided many local men who were willing to play in a football team which took part in friendly matches throughout the 1880/1 season. The first game was held on November 13th, 1880 when the Macclesfield Baptist Church played St Mark's, West Gorton. The Cheshire team won 2-1.

During their second season, 1881/2, the club transferred from Clowes Street to the Kirkmanshulme Cricket Club on Redgate Lane, Gorton. An influx of players from outside the parish of St Mark's meant that the church became less involved with footballing activities. This led to a change in team name from St Mark's (West Gorton) to West Gorton (St Mark's).

The cricket fraternity at the Kirkmanshulme Club disliked the way in which their pitch was ravaged by the West Gorton team, so 1882/3 saw football players having their fixtures at Clemington Park where they won one out of the nine games in that season.

In 1883/4 West Gorton and Gorton Athletic clubs joined forces. This move seemed to pay dividends, and in the early games there were seven victories in eight matches.

A New Name

It soon became clear that a new name was needed for the club, and so in 1884/5 the Gorton Association Football Club emerged, playing its fixtures on a pitch in Pink Bank Lane, Gorton. The winning streak was still in evidence during 1884/5 when 16 games resulted in seven victories, seven drawn matches and just two defeats.

Interestingly, the vice chairman of the newly named club was Mr Beastow, the church warden at St Mark's. He was one of those who instigated the formation of a cricket team in 1879 and a soccer team the following year.

During the mid-1880s Mr Beastow was still passionately involved in soccer when he gave Gorton A.F.C. a set of black football shirts decorated with a white cross.

The club moved from Pink Bank Lane to play their games at a pitch on Reddish Lane

ARDWICK ASSOCIATION FOOTBALL CLUB.

HYDE ROAD HOTEL,
ARDWICK, August 23rd, 1887.

Sir,

Having formed a Club under the above title, and secured a Ground situate between the L. & N. W. Railway and Galloways' Works, in Bennett Street, Hyde Road, we have decided to hold a Meeting in connection with the same, at the above Hotel, on *Tuesday Next, the 30th inst.*, at 8 p.m., prompt.

The bearer of this Circular will be glad to give you all particulars you may require respecting the prospects of the Club.

Hoping you will give this your favourable consideration,

We are, Sir,

Yours respectfully,

W. CHEW, } Hon. Secs.
J. H. WARD, } *Pro Tem.*

N.B.—Your attendance at the Meeting will be greatly esteemed.

---

in the 1885/6 season. They had to pay the landlord of the Bull's Head pub for the use of the land.

Newton Heath Rivalry

The local football scene was given further impetus with the establishment of Newton Heath Football Club, later to become known as Manchester United.

Supporters of both Manchester teams eagerly awaited confrontations between the two clubs. One notable game was a Manchester Cup Series match when Gorton A.F.C. were defeated 11-1 by Newton Heath who subsequently went on to the Final.

Manchester soccer was clearly becoming a popular spectator sport in the 1880s, and during 1887 the Gorton captain, McKenzie, suggested that a piece of waste ground in Ardwick might serve as an ideal venue for Gorton A.F.C.'s games. This was prompted by the fact that the landlord of the Bull's Head was intending to push up the rents on the Reddish Lane ground. In moving, the club was renamed Ardwick F.C.

Ardwick F.C. and Professional Football

The new playing area was adjacent to Bennett Street, Ardwick behind the Hyde Road Hotel, bordered by the forbidding arches of a railway line and gloomy factories. The pub was used for club meetings, with access to the Ardwick club's ground by means of Bennett Street, at the side of the Hyde Road Hotel. This hostelry later became known as the City Gates before its closure in the late 1980s. (See photograph at the end of this chapter.)

Local industries provided help with the construction and improvements of the Ardwick ground. A local brewer, Stephen Chester Thompson, who became president of Ardwick Football Club, paid for the grassed surface and stand.

By now the club had its first professional player, Jack Hodgetts, who received five shillings a week in 1887 (25p). In 1888/9, the opposition comprised mainly local sides from the Manchester area with names such as Heaton Park, Gorton Villa, and of course, Newton Heath.

Ardwick F.C. signed several players from outside Manchester in the early 1890s, including the Scottish quartet of Douglas, Young, Campbell and McWhinnie. Further personnel were recruited from Bolton Wanderers: Rushton, McWhirter, Milne, Haydock, Whittle, Weir and Pearson.

You can imagine the reaction of residents in the drab streets of Ardwick and Gorton when they realised that an English international, David Weir, was playing for the local team.

To give you some idea of the size of the Hyde Road ground, in September 1890 5,000 people turned up to see Blackburn defeat Ardwick 5-1.

The Alliance and the Football League

The Football Combination was established by clubs who failed to gain admittance to the Football League. When it ceased in April 1889, most of the teams became founder members of the Football Alliance.

The 1891/2 season saw Ardwick playing in the Alliance where they finished seventh out of a dozen clubs.

Alliance League - top eight teams 1891/92

Team	Points
Nottingham Forest	33
Newton Heath*	31
Small Heath	29
Sheffield Wednesday	28
Burton Swifts	26
Crewe Alexandra	18
Ardwick	18
Bootle	18

*later to become M/c United

In the Manchester Cup of 1891/2 Ardwick beat Fairfield 4-0, and defeated Bolton in the Final 4-1.

Things were looking good as the Manchester club was admitted to the Second Division of the Football League in 1892. The captain at this period was Dave Russell who had served with Nottingham Forest and Preston.

In Ardwick's first League game, they thrashed Bootle 7-0. Naturally, interest in the

Opposite: Dated August 23rd, 1887, this letter comes from the Hyde Road Hotel, Ardwick. It is an invitation to attend a meeting on August 30th, 1887 at the Hyde Road Hotel, in connection with the formation of Ardwick Football Club.

club blossomed, so that when they finished fifth in the League at the close of the 1892/3 season, some 3,000-4,000 spectators were a common sight at each game.

A Hard Season: 1893/94

The 1893/4 season was a rather traumatic period in the club's history as fears of bankruptcy threatened the future of Ardwick, while performance on the pitch left a lot to be desired.

The club took part in 28 matches, lost 18 and drew 2. This meant re-election with Ardwick F.C. just managing to retain a place in the League, in 13th position.

The whole situation was aggravated by Weir's departure at a time when players such as Davies, Yates and Morris were being sold to raise much needed cash.

Manchester City and Meredith

Salvation came in the form of one Joshua Parlby who was largely responsible for rebuilding the ailing Ardwick soccer club. As a result of his intervention the club became a limited company, and the name was changed to Manchester City.

The first match with the new title was on September 1st, 1894. In this Second Division opening game of the season, the final score read: Bury 4, Manchester City 2.

The 1894/5 season was a milestone in Manchester City's history when one of the club's most important signings, Billy Meredith, joined the squad. Following brief spells with the Welsh side, Chirk, and Cheshire team, Northwich Victoria, this football genius signed for City on 19th October, 1894.

Meredith's first game for his new club was on October 27th, when a close 5-4 defeat for City was the result.

In his first season Billy scored a dozen times. The crowds quickly realised they were watching a soccer maestro with a profound influence on the whole team.

On March 9th and 23rd, 1895, City took on Notts County and Lincoln. The fans were delighted as 18 goals were scored by their club in the two fixtures. Their new hero played a major role in each match, scoring one goal on March 9th, when the result was an impressive 7-1, and two goals in the even more spectacular 11-3 defeat of Lincoln.

Billy Meredith was quite a character with his distinctive short hair cut and a habit of chewing on a toothpick. His illustrious career spanned 30 years, and while with City he won an FA Cup Winners' medal and two Second Division Championship medals. He also scored 145 League goals for City.

During the 1905/6 season, Billy was suspended along with 16 other players and a couple of directors. Details of this are given later.

In 1906, he transferred to rivals Manchester

United, returning to City as player/coach in the 1921/22 season. His last League game for the Blues was on November 4th, 1922, against West Bromwich Albion.

Remarkably, in 1923/4, when Meredith was 50 years old, he played for City in the Round Three Cup tie against Brighton, and again in the Semi-final with Newcastle United on March 29th, 1924.

Test Matches

In 1894/5 City came ninth out of 16 clubs in Division Two when a typical team line up was:

Williams, Smith, Dyer, Mann, Jones, Nash, Finnerhan, Rowan, Wallace, Calvey, Little

The following season brought second position in Division Two with City needing to take part in "Test Matches" which settled promotion. Here is how the club fared in these games:

Test Matches in 1895/96

Date	Opposition	Result
April 18th	West Bromwich Albion	D 1-1
April 20th	West Bromwich Albion	L 1-6
April 25th	Small Heath	W 3-0
April 27th	Small Heath	L 0-8

City were robbed of promotion by the 8-0 defeat even though the club had lost only five League matches while in Division Two, which gave them second place in the table. The Test Matches, however, decided who was promoted.

Local rivals Newton Heath (later to become Manchester United) were fully aware of the Test Match procedure. In their first season in the Football League they were propping up Division One, and had to take part in Test Matches to avoid relegation. The close of the 1893/4 season, however, saw Newton Heath once again at the bottom of the table. This time they were relegated to the Second Division following a 2-0 Test Match defeat by Liverpool on April 28th 1894.

In spite of going down 8-0 in the Test Match, City finished second in Division Two, winning 21 of the 30 games played. Again, in the Manchester Senior Cup, City reached the Final only to be beaten by Bury 2-1 on April 11th, 1896.

Here is how the top of the Second Division looked at the close of the 1895/96 season with City in second place and local rivals Newton Heath positioned sixth.

Top of Division Two 1895/96

	P	W	D	L	F	A	Points
Liverpool	30	22	2	6	106	32	46
Manchester City	30	21	4	5	63	38	46
Grimsby	30	20	2	8	82	38	42
Burton Wanderers	30	19	4	7	69	40	42
Newcastle	30	16	2	12	73	50	34
Newton Heath	30	15	3	12	66	57	33

New Players, Mixed Results

New faces in the squad included Holmes, Gillespie and Ray who moved from Chesterfield, Lincoln and Burslem Port Vale respectively.

Holmes stayed with City from 1896 to 1905 before moving to Clapton Orient, following over 150 appearances. Billy Gillespie remained on the books from 1897 to 1905. A determined centre forward, he scored 132 goals during his 231 games. He was the brother of Matthew Gillespie who represented local rivals Newton Heath between 1896 and 1899.

Ray's previous clubs included Burslem Port Vale and Macclesfield, before his move to City in 1896 with whom he stayed for four years.

Interestingly, during 1897 City signed on two players both with the surname Smith. Walter transferred from Stockport while William arrived from Buxton. Football reports of that era refer to "Buxton Smith" and "Stockport Smith" carrying out their duties for the Manchester club.

1896/97 saw City finish a reasonable sixth in the Second Division, but fans were disappointed with the 6-0 defeat by Preston North End in the FA Cup. The team on January 30th comprised:

Williams, Harper, Ray, Holmes, Mann, McBride, Meredith, Sharples, Foster, Gunn, Lewis

The Round One encounter was attended by 6,000 people, with City fans smarting after the 1-0 defeat on January 16th by Newton Heath in the Manchester Senior Cup.

Still in Division Two, the City squad of 1897/8 performed well, finishing the season in third place. Fans enjoyed the last League game on April 16th when City hammered nine goals past Burton's goalkeeper. Meredith and Whitehead each had hat tricks, Stockport Smith produced two goals, and Gillespie one.

Several matches in the 1897/8 season attracted large crowds, with 20,000 witnessing a 1-1 draw against Newton Heath on October 16th, while a similar number enjoyed the confrontation with second placed Newcastle on March 16th. The Geordies won 2-0.

In the FA Cup, City knocked out Wigan County 1-0 in Round One, but went down 1-0 to Bolton Wanderers in Round Two.

Division Two Champions, 1899

The 1898/99 season was a memorable one as City gained top position in Division Two. Losing only five of 34 League games, the club obtained a record 52 points.

Four of the top six clubs were from the North of England, with Leicester and Walsall representing the Midlands. City and Glossop North End became the first clubs to gain automatic promotion to Division One without having to take part in the Test Matches.

Top of Division Two 1898/99	
Team	Points
Manchester City	52
Glossop N.E.	46
Leicester Fosse	45
Newton Heath	43
New Brighton	43
Walsall	42

Meredith's contribution to City's success was phenomenal. He clearly enjoyed a physical challenge as he displayed a catalogue of hustling moves which fooled opposition defences. During 1898/99, Billy scored 29 goals in 33 League games.

This obviously delighted the fans who were also eager to see how new signing Di Jones would fare. Like Meredith, he had played for the famous Chirk side before joining Bolton and then moving on to City in the 1898 close season. Jones gained a Welsh Cup Winner's medal in 1888 while with the Welsh Club before his transfer to Bolton. Whilst with City, he made 118 appearances.

Into the First Division

In Division One, City finished seventh out of 18 clubs in 1899/1900. Glossop North End could not maintain the required standard and were relegated in the same year.

The Manchester club was now taking on such soccer giants as Liverpool, Newcastle United, Everton and Aston Villa, but financial problems were causing some concern in the late 1890s. However, a series of fund raising activities helped City to secure a stronger bank balance. Again, local brewer, Stephen Chester Thompson injected considerable financial support in return for the sole right to sell his beer at the Hyde Road ground.

The increased cash flow encouraged the club to construct a 75 yard long stand which boosted the ground capacity to 28,000. Division One status seemed to attract larger crowds. For example, on September 9th, 22,000 people witnessed a 4-0 win over Derby County with goals by Meredith (2), Gillespie and Ross. On October 28th, 25,000 saw Liverpool beat City 1-0. One famous visitor to the improved Hyde Road ground was the Prime Minister, A. J. Balfour, who came to Manchester in the Autumn of 1900.

How often does a goalkeeper score a goal? Harry Dowd did in February 1964. This rare event also occurred on April 14th, 1900. City went down 3-1 to Sunderland in a game where the Manchester 'keeper, Charlie Williams, blasted the ball down the pitch. Aided by strong gusts of wind, it beat Scottish international goalkeeper Doig and gave City a consolation goal!

There were quite a few crowd-pullers among the team at the close of the 1890s including Di Jones, Fred Williams, and the former Celtic and Newton Heath forward, Joseph Cassidy. Typical line-ups also included Ray, Moffatt, B. Smith, Holmes, Tonge, Ross, Gillespie, Dougal and S. Smith, as when City met Nottingham Forest in December 1899.

Pictured before its closure in 1988, the City Gates public house, Ardwick was formerly called the Hyde Road Hotel. It played a major role in the early days of Ardwick F.C., acting as a handy meeting place for both fans and players. The Bennett Street football ground was located just behind the pub.

2

The Early 1900s

Division Two Soccer

The dawn of a new century did not offer much in terms of F.A. Cup success for City, who were knocked out by West Bromwich Albion in Round One of the 1900/1 competition.

During the early 1900s new personnel included the powerful Jack Hillman who signed from Burnley in January 1902. The 16-stone six footer remained with City until his move to Millwall in 1906. Local lad Frank Booth, who was born in Hyde, came to City from Stockport County in 1902. He was one of those suspended during the 1906 F.A. investigations (discussed later), finishing his playing days with City in 1912 following the 1908 amnesty. Other examples of new arrivals were a couple of 1902 signings, Drummond and McOustra, who stayed with the club until 1904 and 1907 respectively.

Naturally the fans expected great things from the new players, but the close of the 1900/01 season saw the club positioned eleventh in Division One, dropping to eighteenth in the following year.

In the final League match on April 19th they drew 2-2 with Stoke, and were relegated to Division Two.

The club boasted some competent players and were determined to bounce back to Division One. This they did after losing only five and drawing four matches in 34 League games in 1902/3. City scored a Football League record of 95 goals of which Meredith supplied 22 and Gillespie 30.

Fans were more than pleased with the high-scoring winter games against Burnley, Burslem Port Vale and Gainsborough. The Burnley match on 31st January, 1903 resulted in a 6-0 victory for the Manchester side. A fortnight later they put seven goals past the Burslem Port Vale 'keeper in a match which ended 7-1. On February 28th, City produced another magnificent score, when Gainsborough Trinity were humiliated 9-0.

Many observers attributed much of City's outstanding performance to the new secretary-manager Tom Maley. Taking up his duties in the summer of 1902, he achieved a great deal before becoming involved in the 1906 scandal. He was superseded in that year by Harry Newbould.

Maley had inherited a core of seasoned players like Gillespie, Sandy Turnbull and Meredith, but he supplemented his team by buying new people. These included Booth, Bannister, Burgess and Livingstone.

At 5ft 4ins, Herbert Burgess was the smallest full back ever to represent England. The Openshaw-born stalwart was one of the

1906 suspended players who moved over to Manchester United.

George Livingstone left Liverpool's ranks to play for City in May 1903, returning to his native Scotland in 1907 when he signed for Glasgow Rangers. He orchestrated some outstanding moves while with City and supplied many useful balls to Billy Meredith. The Welsh Wizard was also fed intelligent passes by inside forward Jimmy Bannister who was bought by City in 1902.

The young team soared to the top of Division Two in 1903 while the newly-named Manchester United (formerly Newton Heath) occupied fifth place.

The impressive League position, and the subsequent move up to Division One was the result of a concerted effort by both the team and the new board of directors. Particular mention ought to be made of the contributions of Meredith and Gillespie who scored in 23 of the 34 League games in that season.

Top of Division Two 1902/03

	P	W	D	L	F	A	Pts
Manchester City	34	25	4	5	95	29	54
Small Heath	34	24	3	7	74	36	51
Woolwich Arsenal	34	20	8	6	66	30	48
Bristol City	34	17	8	9	59	38	42
Manchester United	34	15	8	11	53	38	38
Chesterfield	34	14	9	11	67	40	37

Almost "The Double"

In 1903/04, City finished second in Division One and also reached the FA Cup Final!

The League

What an enjoyable season as City won their first four games during September 1903. Stoke were defeated 2-1, Derby went under by the same score, Wolves were beaten 4-1, while Notts County were dismissed 3-0.

Larger crowds were attracted to the Hyde Road ground. For example, 28,000 watched the match against Sheffield United on October 3rd, and 30,000 attended the victory over Aston Villa in the same month. A crowd of 35,000 saw City lose 5-3 to Sheffield United in December 1903.

April 23rd, 1904 was an eventful, if not fretful, day for fans. City were playing in the FA Cup Final, and a close watch was being kept on The Wednesday -v- Aston Villa League game, scheduled for the same day. If the Yorkshire club had lost, City would need one more win to land the Championship trophy. However, Aston Villa were defeated 4-2, and a couple of days later the Manchester club went down 0-1 to Everton in the last match of the season. The Wednesday had gained the championship by just three points!

The City faithful had hoped that their team could climb up the table and secure top place, but they were not disappointed by the overall performance – 34 League games were played in 1903/04 of which City lost only nine, drew six and won 19.

Moments to Remember

Top of Division One 1903/04

	P	W	D	L	F	A	Pts
The Wednesday	34	20	7	7	48	28	47
Manchester City	34	19	6	9	71	45	44
Everton	34	19	5	10	59	32	43
Newcastle	34	18	6	10	58	45	42
Aston Villa	34	17	7	10	70	48	41
Sunderland	34	17	5	12	63	49	39

Consolation appeared in the form of FA Cup success when the club won the trophy for the first time. The next couple of seasons would prove quite successful too, as City came third and then fifth in the League.

The FA Cup

Before 1904, City had experienced little success at a national level, so we can imagine the elation of fans as their team performed competently in the League and also took part in the FA Cup Final.

Clearly Turnbull, Gillespie and Meredith played a major role in City's reaching the Final. They made significant contributions in League games too. During the season Turnbull scored 16 goals, Gillespie 18, and Meredith, 11.

The three stars obviously found places on the FA Cup Final team which comprised:

Hillman, McMahon, Burgess, Frost, Hynds, Ashworth, Meredith, Livingstone, Gillespie, Turnbull, Booth

Just over 61,000 attended the Crystal Palace venue where City defeated Bolton Wanderers with a controversial Billy Meredith goal.

Bolton fans thought he was offside when he received a Livingstone pass. Meredith weaved among several defenders and then banged in the ball from 12 yards. The referee did not blow for offside, and so the score of 1-0 meant that Billy Meredith received the FA Cup from Lord Alfred Lyttelton.

City had to wait another 30 years before winning the FA Cup again, although they were runners-up in 1926 and 1933.

As a footnote – the price of a 1904 Cup Final ticket was just five shillings (25p) in the uncovered stands.

Route to the 1904 FA Cup Final

Round	Opponents	Result	Scorers
1	Sunderland	3-2	Turnbull (2); Gillespie
2	Woolwich Arsenal	2-0	Turnbull; Booth
3	Middlesbrough	0-0	
3(Replay)	Middlesbrough	3-1	Livingstone; Gillespie; Turnbull
Semi-final	The Wednesday (At Goodison Park)	3-1	Meredith; Gillespie; Turnbull
Final	Bolton Wanderers (At the Crystal Palace)	1-0	Meredith

Suspensions and Fines

A dismal chapter in the City story began to unfold in 1905 when Billy Meredith was suspended from April 29th, 1905 for a year, for allegedly offering a bribe to an Aston Villa player in a crucial League game.

The Villa man reported the incident to the FA who began an investigation of the Hyde Road club. It became clear that there was evidence of illegal payments and bonuses at the City club, and 17 City players were banned from May 1906 until January the following year.

The club put these men up for sale, and Manchester United secretary-manager Ernest Mangnall snapped up Herbert Burgess, Sandy Turnbull and Jimmy Bannister. George Livingstone moved from City to United at a later date, following a spell with Glasgow Rangers whom he joined in January 1907.

In addition to the punishment meted out to the City players, secretary-manager Maley and former chairman W. Forrest were suspended along with directors Davies and Allison.

The reshuffle of personnel meant that Harry Newbould took over as City's secretary-manager in July 1906, remaining for six years. On top of all the suspensions, the club was fined £250 while players were ordered to pay a total of £900.

Could City survive this trauma?

The fans waited anxiously, but their club finished a respectable third in the 1904/5 Division One table at the end of a controversial season.

A grim task faced new secretary-manager Harry Newbould who had to rebuild a depleted team. He began by signing on such new players as Eadie and Grieve from Greenock Morton in 1906. They joined another recent Scottish acquisition, left-half Banks, who had moved from Kilmarnock in December 1905.

Harry Newbould created a formidable forward line comprising a number of international players. George Stewart played for Scotland, Conlin and Thornley represented England, and Billy L. Jones was a Welsh international.

Finishing fifth in Division One, City had little else to boast about in 1906. On January 15th, they were eliminated from the FA Cup in Round One when Sheffield United won 4-1.

City – United Rivalry 1906-8

When Manchester United entered Division One in the 1906/7 season, Mancunians wondered how the two clubs would progress. City had 16 goals hammered past them in their first three matches of September 1906:

Date	Opponents	Score
Sept 1st	Woolwich Arsenal	Lost 4-1
Sept 3rd	Everton	Lost 9-1
Sept 8th	Sheffield Wednesday	Lost 3-1

Moments to Remember

The first of these games left City with just six men, as the remainder succumbed to a sweltering heatwave which made it 90 degrees in the shade.

Before 1905/06 City had met Newton Heath on ten occasions, playing the renamed Manchester United in 1902/03. These had all been Division Two games, the first top Division clash occurring on December 1st, 1906 when United lost 3-0.

Alongside is how things turned out between 1894 and 1908.

City accomplished little in the 1907 FA Cup, a 2-2 draw resulting from the January 12th meeting with Blackburn Rovers, while the replay saw City knocked out of the competition 1-0.

New signings involved Walter Smith from Leicester Fosse in July 1906, and David Ross from Norwich in February the following year.

Following their turbulent time in 1906, City seemed to follow a more normal routine in 1907/8, reaching third place in Division One.

A crucial game in this season was the April 18th meeting of the two Manchester clubs. Before the match City were in the runners-up position, but the 0-0 draw and the same score for the next two games put them third in League Division One. Little wonder a crowd of 40,000 turned out to the Ardwick ground to watch the Manchester derby.

The FA Cup eluded City, as Second Division Fulham eliminated them in a Third Round replay (3-1) on January 26th, 1908.

City-v-United 1894-1908

Division Two

1894/5	City	2
	Newton Heath	5
	Newton Heath	4
	City	1
1895/6	Newton Heath	1
	City	1
	City	2
	Newton Heath	1
1896/7	City	0
	Newton Heath	0
	Newton Heath	2
	City	1
1897/8	Newton Heath	1
	City	1
	City	0
	Newton Heath	1
1898/9	Newton Heath	3
	City	0
	City	4
	Newton Heath	0
1902/3	Manchester United	1
	City	1
	City	0
	Manchester United	2

Division One

1906/7	City	3
	Manchester United	0
	Manchester United	1
	City	1
1907/8	Manchester United	3
	City	1
	City	0
	Manchester United	0

Top of Division One 1907/08

	P	W	D	L	F	A	Pts
Manchester United	38	23	6	9	81	48	52
Aston Villa	38	17	9	12	77	59	43
Manchester City	38	16	11	11	62	54	43
Newcastle	38	15	12	11	65	54	42
Wednesday	38	19	4	15	73	64	42
Middlesbrough	38	17	7	14	54	45	41

Manchester City

The 1906 City players line up in front of the refreshment bar. In the all-male crowd, everyone is wearing a cap.

Large Crowds

At the close of the 1907/8 season the club finished a respectable third in Division One, but a year later they plummeted to second from the bottom.

Relegation followed, with 1909/10 bringing City into contact with such Division Two clubs as Stockport and Oldham.

Nevertheless, the club still attracted large-crowds. In December 1908, 40,000 spectators witnessed the 2-1 defeat of Chelsea, while a similar number watched the January 1909 confrontation with Manchester United when City went down 3-1.

One reason for the large crowds was the entertaining soccer provided by Tom Holford. His League debut for City was in April

1908, and in January the following year he scored three hat-tricks! He was hungry for goals, with another trio against The Wednesday on March 27th, 1909. City won 4-0, with the other goal coming from Jones.

Representing City between 1907 and 1913, wing-half Tom Holford took part in 184 League and Cup games, scoring a total of 38 goals.

Top of Division Two 1909/10

	P	W	D	L	F	A	Pts
Manchester City	38	23	8	7	81	40	54
Oldham	38	23	7	8	79	39	53
Hull City	38	23	7	8	80	46	53
Derby	38	22	9	7	72	47	53
Leicester Fosse	38	20	4	14	79	58	44
Glossop North End	38	18	7	13	64	57	43

Holford's hat-tricks 1909

Date	Opposition	Result	Scorers
January 9th	Bradford City (League game)	W.4-3	Holford(3); Conlin
January 16th	Tottenham Hotspur (FA Cup)	L.3-4	Holford (3)
January 30th	Everton (League game)	W.4-0	Holford (3); Wilkinson
March 27th	The Wednesday (League Game)	W.4-0	Holford (3) Jones

Relegation and Recovery

In the 1908/09 season, City were relegated to Division Two but they soon shot back to the First Division, having lost only seven of the 38 League matches played in the lower reaches of the Football League.

During the summer of 1910 the club provided more covered accommodation at a cost of £3,000. This meant that 35,000 spectators were now protected from the elements at the Hyde Road ground.

Large numbers turned out to see how City would perform on their return to Division One in the 1910/11 season. For example, the September fixtures with Notts. County, Manchester United and Liverpool attracted 30,000, 60,000 and 40,000 respectively.

For all their efforts, City did not accomplish much in terms of League or FA Cup success. The club finished seventeenth out of 20 in Division One, while Wolves pushed them out of the FA Cup in Round Two (1-0).

September 1911 opened a new season with fans hoping that City would improve on the previous year's performance. However, there were only five wins in the first 28 League games, January and February being particularly dismal as City did not win once in the League. They did, however, beat Preston North End (1-0) in the FA Cup, but Round Two saw City go down 1-0 to Oldham Athletic.

Manchester City

In the 1909/10 season, City embarked on a Continental tour taking in a number of countries. The front cover of the tour booklet, shown here, depicts the Manchester coat of arms and carries the date, May 10th 1910. We also see the name of the chairman, W. A. Wilkinson, and secretary H.J. Newbould.

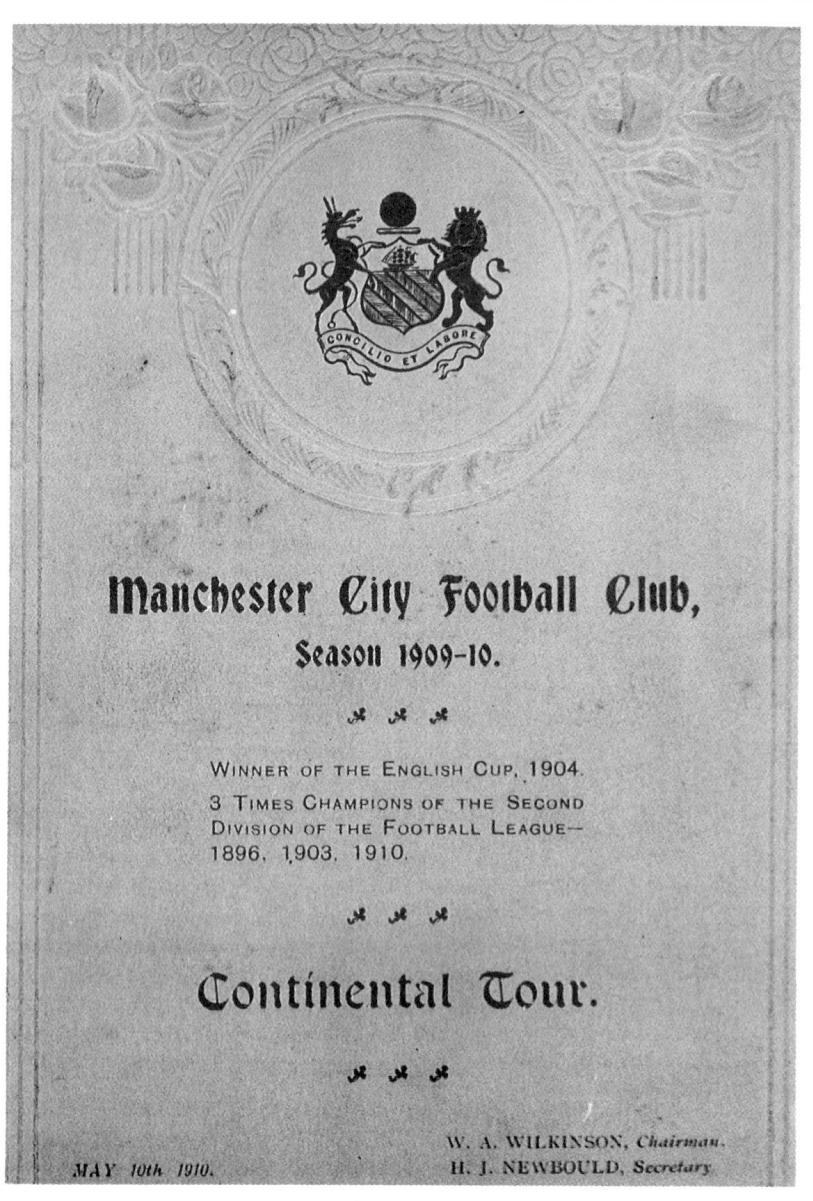

Moments to Remember

The second page of Manchester City's Continental tour programme of 1910.

Itinerary.

Tuesday, May 10th.
  Manchester, depart (London Rd.)   5-0 p.m.
  London, arrive ... ... 9-55 ,,
    Headquarters: The Howard Hotel.

Wednesday, May 11th.
  London, depart (Charing Cross) ... 9-0 a.m.
  Dover   ,, ... 11-0 ,,
  Ostend, arrive ... ... 2-0 p.m.
  Ostend, depart ... ... 3-20 ,,
  Brussels, arrive (Nord) ... ... 5-20 ,,
    Headquarters: Grand Hotel.

Thursday, May 12th.
  Visit the Exhibition and the Field of Waterloo.

Friday, May 13th.
  Brussels, depart (Nord) ... ... 5-0 ,,
  Cologne, arrive (Hauptbahnhof) ...11-1 ,,

Saturday, May 14th.
  Cologne, depart (sleeping car) ...11-27 ,,

Sunday, May 15th.
  Hamburg, arrive ... ... 6-55 a.m.
    Headquarters: Hotel Streit.

Manchester City

Harry Newbould was manager when this 1910 club photograph was taken. In charge from 1906-1912, he is on the seated row, wearing a tie, fifth from the left. The year 1910 was a significant milestone in the City story. Enjoying territorial and numerical supremacy in most of their games, the team became Division Two Champions for the third time. City had previously won the Trophy in 1899 and 1903.

W.A.Smith, W.Bottomley, R.Humphries, G.Dorsett. R.Coding

R.Iles (Asst.Trainer), F.Norgrove, J.Wilkinson, F.Kelso, J.Lyall, H.Jackson, C.Burgess, W.Eadie, R.Chatt (Trainer)

J. Buchan, H.Bentley, G.Stewart, W.Humphries, H.J.Newbould, W.Gould, W.L.Jones, J.W.Smith, T.Holford, H.Carlton

G.Wynn, (Sec.) D.Ross, J.Conlin

One remarkable occasion was the embarrassing situation on January 27th, 1912 when City missed three penalties! In a 1-1 draw with Newcastle United, Wynn provided the only goal for the Hyde Road club.

They finished fifteenth out of twenty clubs in Division One. Fans were naturally despondent – particularly since they had hoped for an improvement in performance following the signing of two players. In November 1911, Young had moved north to City from Spurs, while Henry came from Leicester Fosse.

Manager Mangnall

The media had a field day when Manchester United's Ernest Mangnall moved to City in September 1912. Joining the club as secretary-manager, he was determined to keep City in Division One. Interestingly, it was he who had pounced on Billy Meredith, Sandy Turnbull, Herbert Burgess and Jimmy Bannister in 1907 after the suspension scandal.

This successor to Harry Newbould remained with City until 1924, and died in 1932.

Naturally enough, the Manchester football community eagerly awaited the derby clashes – especially since there had been such an interchange of playing and managerial personnel.

Here is what happened in 1912/13:

City-v-United 1912/3			
Date	Result	Scorers	Crowd
Sept 7th	Manchester United 0		
	Manchester City 1	Wynn	38,900
December 28th	Manchester United 2	West (2)	36,220
	Manchester City 0		

In Mangnall's first year with City, his team finished the season in sixth place. No doubt he had his hands full with the commotion surrounding the Second Round of the FA Cup.

On January 11th, 1913, City defeated Birmingham 4-0 in Round One and the subsequent match was held on February 1st. The Hyde Road ground was the venue for the tie with Sunderland. Official figures gave the attendance as 41,709, but some sources claimed there were 50,000 people inside the ground while a further 15,000 waited outside.

The spectators were crammed into the terraces and people began spilling on to the pitch. As a result, the game was abandoned during extra time, when the score was 0-0. The F.A. fined City £500, and the Manchester club lost 2-0 in the replay at Sunderland on February 5th.

New acquisitions about this period included Welsh international goalkeeper Edwin Hughes, a further 'keeper Goodchild, plus Howard, who joined the club in September 1912.

The first of these remained with City from 1912 to 1920, following his move from Wrexham, while Goodchild represented the club between 1911 and 1927, becoming the regular goalie after the first World War. What a debut for Howard in January 1913 when he scored all four goals in the 4-1 victory over Liverpool! This was clearly a good omen, since between 1912 and 1920, he put away a total of 43 goals.

The First World War

With war looming, City found themselves thirteenth in Division One at the close of the 1913/4 season. March seemed to be dominated by games with the two Sheffield clubs, and Manchester City reached Round Four of the FA Cup before being eliminated by Sheffield United after two replays.

City -v- Sheffield teams, March 1914			
Date	Competition	Opponents	Result
March 7th	FA Cup, Round Four	Sheffield United	0-0
March 12th	FA Cup Round Four, (Replay)	Sheffield United	0-0
March 14th	League game	The Wednesday	2-2
March 16th	FA Cup Round Four (Second Replay)	Sheffield United	0-1

The club introduced several new names such as Hanney from Reading (£1,200), Browell who was with Everton, and Horace Barnes, who cost City £2,500 when they bought him from Derby County.

Manchester City

Right: an extract from a City-v-United programme in 1914 where the pencil alterations indicate late team changes for the Reds. One interesting name on the United side is outside-right Billy Meredith.

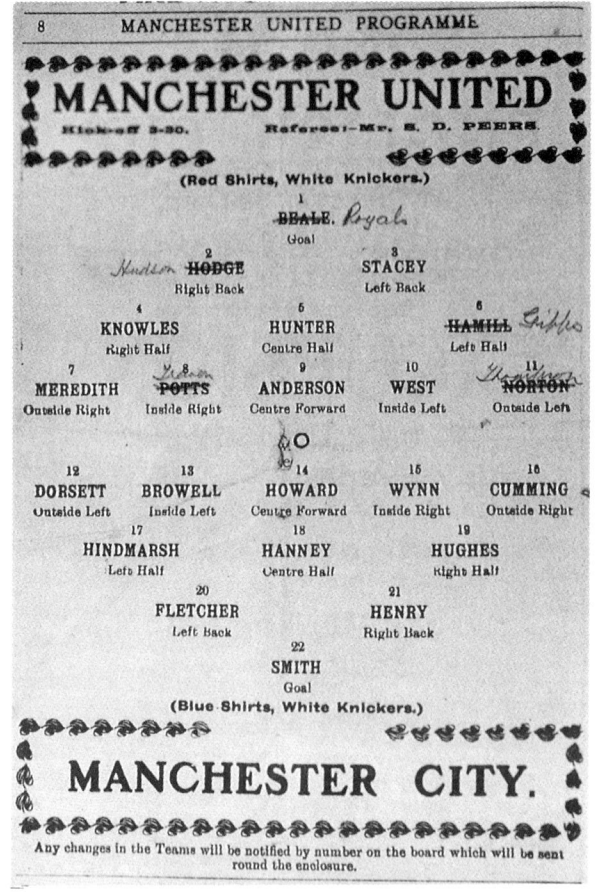

Like Browell, he became a prolific scorer, with 125 goals in 235 League and FA Cup appearances. Tommy Browell moved to Manchester from the Merseyside club for a £1,780 fee, and his contributions were decisive to say the least. He netted 139 goals in 247 League and FA Cup matches.

A typical City side in 1914 was the team defeated 1-0 by Sheffield United on March 16th in Round Four of the F.A. Cup:

Smith, Henry, Fletcher, Hughes,, Hanney, Hindmarsh, Jones, Taylor, Howard, Browell, Williams

At one stage in 1914/15, City were fifth in Division One, while local rivals Oldham were second. In 1915, April 5th brought a crucial game between the two clubs which resulted in a 0-0 draw. None of City's four remaining League games produced a win, the club gaining only two points from their last five matches.

Manchester United, meanwhile, were in the doldrums – eighteenth out of 20 clubs.

During World War One the full League programme was suspended and clubs took part in regional competitions. City did well, finishing in the top five clubs each season during the war.

Top of Division One 1914/15

	P	W	D	L	F	A	Pts
Everton	38	19	8	11	76	47	46
Oldham	38	17	11	10	70	56	45
Blackburn	38	18	7	13	83	61	43
Burnley	38	18	7	13	61	47	43
Manchester City	38	15	13	10	49	39	43
Sheffield United	38	15	13	10	49	41	43

Several players were called up to fight for their country, including J. Brennan, W.L. Jones and T. Broad.

A significant event occurred towards the end of the war when, in 1917, City put the lease of the Hyde Road ground in their own name. Before this it was held between Chester's Brewery and the Manchester, Sheffield and Lincolnshire Railway Company with City being sub-tenants.

After the War

When normal soccer returned to Hyde Road after the war, only four years of the lease were left, and discussions took place concerning a move to a new ground.

An important visitor to Hyde Road was King George V who attended on March 27th 1920. He saw the home team beat Liverpool 2-1 as Horace Barnes delivered the killer blow with his two goals in front of almost 40,000 spectators. The City star scored 23 goals in League and FA Cup matches during the 1919/20 season.

So, in the first full season following the war, City finished seventh in Division One. The fans had only a brief look at 1919 signings Lamph and Goodwin who both departed before the end of the 1921 season. Another to leave was Teddy Hanney, transferring to Coventry for a £2,000 fee in 1919 following six years with the Manchester club.

The 1919/20 period proved to be a financial success for the club, partly as a result of fees received when players were sold.

The Fire

1920/21 – what a season to enjoy in terms of League success! City did not suffer a single home defeat, and after their last match on May 7th, 1921, they were second in Division One, just behind Burnley. United were 13th out of 22 clubs.

Top of Division One 1920/21

	P	W	D	L	F	A	Pts
Burnley	42	23	13	6	79	36	59
Manchester City	42	24	6	12	70	50	54
Bolton	42	19	14	9	77	53	52

By now it was quite commonplace to find large crowds at the Hyde Road ground, with many games attracting at least 30,000 spectators. In fact, 40,000 watched the 3-1 victory over Aston Villa on August 30th, 1920, while a similar number witnessed the 3-0 defeat of Manchester United on November 27th. A week before, 66,000 spectators had gone to United's ground and enjoyed seeing the two Manchester giants confront each other in a 1-1 draw.

FA Cup Matches 1921/22

Date	Round	Opponents	Result	Scorers
Jan 7th	One	Darlington	3-1	Browell (3)
Jan 28th	Two	Bolton Wanderers	3-1	Browell (2); Kelly
Feb 18th	Three	Tottenham Hotspur	1-2	Kelly

Manchester City

King George V is pictured visiting the Hyde Road ground in 1920. City played here between 1887 and 1923 before the move to Maine Road.

A fire on the night of November 6th, 1920 destroyed City's only stand at the Hyde Road ground along with many club records. Lorry loads of cinders were hastily sent to the ground as an interim measure, so that a raised section could replace the stand.

City seemed to be undaunted by the blaze and, in the week after it broke out, they dispatched Huddersfield 3-2 at home. Increased success plus the fire again encouraged talk of moving to a new ground. The nearby Belle Vue Pleasure Park was considered, but experts felt it was too small.

In the first eight home games of 1921/22, City were not defeated once, but Bolton put an end to this successful run with their 3-2 victory on December 3rd. Some consolation for the fans was that all 20 home League games in 1920/21 and the first eight the following season did not produce a single defeat until the Bolton game. This was the first home defeat for two years.

City were placed tenth in Division One at the close of the 1922 season with much of the credit going to the proven masters Browell and Barnes. Their emphatic strikes on opposition goalmouths paid off as, between them, they scored in 25 out of 42 League games in 1921/22. Browell netted five goals during City's FA Cup matches.

Maine Road Move

Two major highlights of the 1922/23 season were the construction of the new ground and changes in personnel.

The lease of the Hyde Road ground was due to expire, and the neighbouring tramways department needed the space for a modernisation and expansion programme.

City began looking around, and eventually decided on a $16\frac{1}{4}$ acre site in Moss Side for which they paid £5,500.

They were now in a position to build the largest stadium in England, with the exception of Wembley, which had just been completed after 300 days of hard work.

The contractors McAlpine and Sons were given the task of constructing City's new football ground at Maine Road. Thousands of tons of soil were deposited on a cinder base and then covered with a layer of fertile soil brought from Poynton, Cheshire. The eventual cost was more than £100,000 for a stadium designed to accommodate 90,000 spectators.

The first game at Maine Road took place on August 25th, 1923 when City defeated Sheffield United 2-1 thanks to goals by Barnes and Johnson. Almost 57,000 people enjoyed the match in the new surroundings, including Manchester's Lord Mayor who was introduced to the teams before the game – see the photograph overleaf.

New Manager, 1924

City came eighth in Division One at the close of the 1922/3 season, and were eleventh the next year.

In 1924, secretary-manager Mangnall was succeeded by David Ashworth. Having been

Manchester City

in control for almost 12 years, Mangnall was the inspiration behind the establishment of the Central League and was also a prime mover in the setting up of a Football Manager's Association.

The new manager had been the driving force behind Liverpool's First Division title in 1921/22, and so the fans expected a great deal from him.

Player Mickey Hamill left in the summer of 1924 to try his fortunes with an American soccer club. The Belfast born wing-half had made 128 appearances with City since 1920.

The FA Cup and Meredith's Return

1923/4 was an important period in terms of the F.A. Cup. City defeated Nottingham Forest, and then battled it out with Halifax Town in Round Two until they won after two replays.

The Manchester club pushed out Brighton and Hove Albion from the competition together with Cardiff City. The momentous Semi-final with Newcastle United occurred on March 29th, 1924. Wearing scarlet shirts, City had included the experienced Billy Meredith in the team:

Mitchell, Cookson, Fletcher, Hamill, Pringle, Wilson, Meredith, Roberts, Browell, Barnes, Johnson

Even though he was 50 years old, the Welsh Wizard was chosen as outside right. Meredith had not played in Division One games for several months but had turned out with the Central League side. Billy had been called up to the City squad for the Third Round tie against Brighton, and he played in the three subsequent FA Cup ties.

The fans were hoping that Meredith's accurate centres could provide opportunities for forwards to hammer home the winning goals. He did not let them down. In the Round Four replay against Cardiff on March 12th, Meredith supplied the all-important pass for Browell to score the only goal of the game.

The semi-final, against Newcastle United

Below: Maine Road football stadium opened in 1923. Here the Lord Mayor of Manchester is being introduced to the City squad by Max Woosnam before the inaugural game on August 25th of that year.

Moments to Remember

The year is 1923 and City's outside-left, Murphy, is seen heading towards the Newcastle goal. The two clubs met on April 28th and May 5th, 1923, when the scores were 0-0 and 1-3 in favour of the North East side. The second of these fixtures was City's last League game of the 1922/3 season.

Manchester City

Sam Cowan (left) came to City in 1924 from Doncaster Rovers, having earlier represented Ardwick Juniors, Bullcroft Colliery and Denaby United. This outstanding centre-half was renowned for his aerial ability. The driving force behind the Blues for a decade, he represented the Manchester club in 369 League and 38 Cup fixtures.

was Billy Meredith's last game for City. Sadly it resulted in a 2-0 defeat.

Coincidentally, the Welsh star's League debut for City had been in a game against Newcastle on October 27th, 1894 when the Manchester team lost 4-5.

On April 25th 1925, 15,000 people attended Meredith's Testimonial game at Maine Road where a Glasgow XI challenged a Manchester team. Needless to say the 50-year-old 'Lloyd George of Welsh Football' took part.

Departures and Arrivals, 1924/25

Several players left in the 1920s. Two were university graduates. Max Woosnam had studied at Cambridge where he received sporting honours for soccer, golf and tennis. This robust player remained with City from 1919 to 1925 and took part in a total of 93 games, at one stage captaining England. Woosnam signed for Northwich Victoria in October 1925.

Goalkeeper J. F. Mitchell, a Manchester University graduate, was a teacher when he joined City as an amateur. He turned out for the club on 99 occasions between 1922 and 1926.

1925 saw the departure of outside left William Murphy who had joined the club in 1918. Horace Barnes transferred to Preston in November 1924, having made 235 League and Cup appearances in the decade. He remained with City after joining in 1914.

New blood arrived on the City scene in the shape of Cowan (1924-35), Austin (1924-31) and Hicks (1923-8). The last two players occupied wing positions, with Austin facing the difficult task of taking over from the mighty Meredith. This he did in no uncertain manner during his 172 games with City.

Following Woosnam's departure, Sam Cowan assumed the centre half role, representing the club in three FA Cup Finals in this position. He transferred to Bradford City in 1935 before briefly returning to Maine Road as manager a decade later when he took the club into Division One.

The season was eventful for Frank Roberts who played his initial League game for City in October 1922. This former Bolton Wanderers star received his first England cap in 1924 against Belgium.

During the early games of the 1924/25 season the headlines belonged to Roberts. He scored two goals in each of the games against Bury, Liverpool, Newcastle United and West Ham, and put one away against Nottingham Forest. As if this were not enough, he notched up a hat trick in the Sheffield United game, the seventh match of the season. Roberts was indeed a pleasure to watch as his speed off the mark left defenders helpless. This helped in City's overall League performance as they finished tenth in Division One.

Manchester City

It is April 24th, 1926, FA Cup final day, and City's captain, McMullan (right), shakes hands with Bolton's Smith. Bolton eventually triumphed 1-0. McMullan represented his club in 242 League and FA Cup games between 1926 and 1933.

Relegation

There was considerable drama at the close of the 1925/26 season. Within a seven day period, City were playing in the F.A. Cup Final at Wembley then fighting for a point to avoid relegation to Division Two!

On top of this, manager Ashworth resigned in November 1925 as City struggled to keep their head above water. The successor, Peter Hodge who remained until 1932, played a key role in climaxing City's comeback, leading the club to promotion in 1927/28.

City took part in 42 League games during 1925/26. They lost 19, drew 11 and won 12.

When City played at Wembley on April 24th in the F.A. Cup Final they were fourth from the bottom of Division One, with just one point more than Burnley and Leeds.

The crucial League game was an away fixture at Newcastle when the Tynesiders' opening goal was provided by Gallacher in the first 60 seconds. Roberts netted the equaliser, but Gallacher scored for the second time in the fiftieth minute. City seemed to have little chance of improving on the 2-1 scoreline.

Suddenly, the Manchester club were awarded a penalty and things looked good. It could only happen to City – the Newcastle 'keeper managed to save the spot kick.

It was that man Gallacher again who headed his third goal, and just three minutes from the final whistle, Browell's contribution made it 3-2.

City's newly appointed manager Peter Hodge had plenty to brood on as the team journeyed back to Manchester. Manager and fans eagerly awaited those all-important results from the basement clubs in Division One. Leeds and Burnley had both won their home games, and so City were relegated to Division Two along with Notts. County.

City -v- United, 1925/26

City confronted neighbours United on three occasions during 1925/26 – twice in the League and once in the FA Cup. The Maine Road club won twice, while one game finished in a draw. Who could forget that match on January 23rd, 1926 when City trounced the Reds 6-1? Goals were provided by Austin (2), Roberts (2), Johnson and Hicks as they penetrated the porous United defence.

The crowds were frequently treated to some enterprising play by Austin, who in 1925/26 put away 12 League and three FA Cup goals. Meanwhile, the prolific Roberts scored 21 League and nine FA Cup goals in the same season.

In the other two meetings of the Manchester giants, a 1-1 draw ensued in a September League game, while in the FA Cup Semi-final, the Maine Road side won 3-0.

In addition to a new manager, Peter Hodge, City took on a couple of players – Philip McCloy and left half Jimmy McMullan. The first of these transferred from Ayr in August

Manchester City

Opposite: The 1926 Wembley Cup Final as City tackle Bolton. The Blues were fighting relegation at the time while their opponents occupied a comfortable place in the top half of Division One. A crowd of almost 91,500 saw City beaten 1-0.

1925, proving to be a tough defender who made 157 appearances before moving to Chester in 1930.

Scottish international McMullan was in fact Matt Busby's uncle and, like him, Jimmy started his soccer career with Denny Hibernian. McMullan represented City in 242 games including two Cup Finals, transferring to Oldham as player manager in 1933.

The Road to Wembley: 1926

City's first game was against the renowned amateur team Corinthians at Crystal Palace. The 3-3 draw on January 9th needed a replay which resulted in a 4-0 victory for City. Huddersfield Town were then thrashed by the same score in front of 75,500 at Maine Road.

In the February 1926 tie with Crystal Palace, the Blues, who had faced that replay with the amateurs, Corinthians, hammered in 11 goals against Crystal Palace. In this incredible game, City were leading 7-0 at half time.

Second Division Clapton were vanquished in Round Six of the F.A. Cup, and then it was the all-Manchester Semi-final.

The exciting game took place at Bramall Lane, Sheffield, where Browell put away a couple of goals, and Roberts also scored in the impressive 3-0 victory over United.

The scene was set for the Final against Bolton Wanderers at Wembley.

Route to the 1926 FA Cup Final

Date	Round	Opposition	Result	Scorers
January 9th	3	Corinthians	3-3	Cookson; Roberts; Hicks
January 13th	3(Replay)	Corinthians	4-0	Austin (2); Johnson; Hicks
January 30th	4	Huddersfield Town	4-0	Hicks (2); Browell; Roberts
February 20th	5	Crystal Palace	11-4	Roberts (5); Browell (3); Austin; Johnson; Hicks
March 6th	6	Clapton Orient	6-1	Johnson (3); Hicks; Roberts; Browell
March 27th	Semi-final	Manchester United	3-0	Browell (2); Roberts

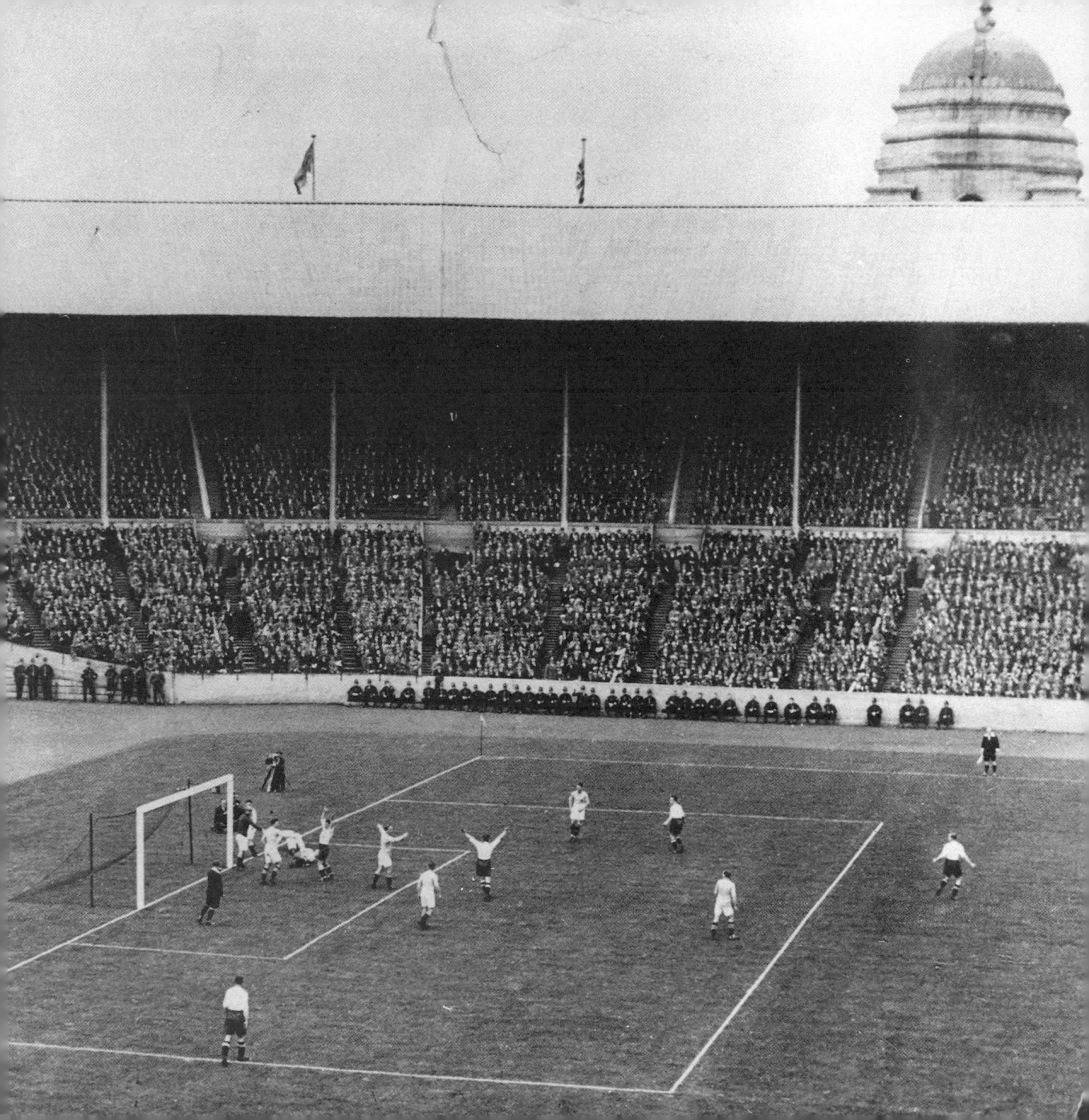

The FA Cup Final – 1926

City were in the FA Cup Final again with Bolton as their opponents. The two clubs had met in similar circumstances in 1904, City winning 1-0 thanks to Meredith's goal.

As the Final drew near, many people favoured Bolton who were higher up Division One than City.

This was the team which represented the Maine Road club on April 24th, 1926 at Wembley:

> Goodchild, Cookson, McCloy, Pringle, Cowan, McMullan, Austin, Browell, Roberts, Johnson and Hicks.

Bolton were in control for the first 20 minutes or so, and at half time there was no score, the game being a story of ebb and flow.

However, the seventy-seventh minute brought the decisive goal as Ted Vizard floated across a centre allowing David Jack to strike with his left foot.

The final score read: Bolton Wanderers 1, Manchester City 0. This was a depressing result for the fans who in the next week would see City go down 3-2 to Newcastle in the last game of the season. As if to rub salt in the wounds, City missed a penalty. The Manchester goals were scored by the tireless pair, Browell and Roberts. At the end of the season, the Blues were relegated, while Bolton finished eighth.

Struggle for Promotion

One has to admire the devotion of City fans in the late 1920s. Their team just missed out on promotion from Division Two in 1927, finishing third in the League when goal average was the deciding factor for movement to the First Division.

Imagine the tension on the morning of the last Saturday in the 1926/27 League calendar when the Maine Road club and Portsmouth were level on points. Both were to end the season with home games.

So, on a warm May 7th, 1927, a 50,000 crowd packed into Maine Road. It seemed too good to be true as the final score read City 8, Bradford 0, with goals from Johnson (3), Broadhurst (2), Hicks, Bell and Roberts. Surely promotion would follow with the high goal average of 1.7705.

But Portsmouth too were pulling out all the stops, thrashing Preston 5-1. This gave them a goal average of 1.7755. Consequently they were promoted on the basis of a 200th part of a goal!

Top of Division Two 1927

	P	W	D	L	F	A	Pts
Middlesbrough	42	27	8	7	122	60	62
Portsmouth	42	23	8	11	87	49	54
Manchester City	42	22	10	10	108	61	54

This unbelievable statistic meant that five thousandths of a goal kept City in Division Two, when one more goal would have guaranteed promotion.

One consolation for the fans was that City's 108 League goals in 1926/27 had made them an attractive side to watch.

Following a decade with Manchester City, right back Sam Cookson transferred to Barnsley in 1928, staying with the Yorkshire club for a couple of seasons before hanging up his boots. Captain Charlie Pringle also departed in 1928. This son-in-law of Billy Meredith contributed much in centre half and wing half roles, making a total of 216 appearances in F.A. Cup and League matches. 1927 brought Andrew Gray from Oldham, the goalkeeper staying with City for three years before moving to Coventry City.

There was joy at last for the Maine Road faithful as their team held on to the top place in Division Two in 1928, thus guaranteeing promotion. Clearly City had the tenacity required of teams capable of winning the Championship, and this attracted the crowds. This was reflected by an average gate of 38,000 in 1927/28.

The Maine Road side completed the 1927/28 season two points ahead of Leeds United, and scored 100 goals. The Yorkshire club was also seeking promotion, and met City on September 17th and April 25th when the Maine Road team won on both occasions.

The two adversaries met again in an FA Cup game on January 16th where City won 1-0 in an exciting match when injured 'keeper Gray was replaced by winger Austin. City went on to defeat Sunderland before losing 1-0 to Stoke City in Round Five.

Tommy Johnson and Matt Busby

Back in Divsion One, City scored a creditable 95 goals of which 38 were attributed to soccer ace Tommy Johnson. Examples of his scoring prowess included five goals in the 6-2 demolition of Everton on September 15th when City's other goal was put in the net by Brook.

Newcomers to Maine Road at the close of the 1920s included Billy Felton, formerly of Sheffield Wednesday. He remained until 1932, playing 73 League and 10 FA Cup games. Halifax released goalkeeper Barber for £1,000 in 1927 and he stayed with Manchester City until his retirement in 1932. In March 1928, Eric Brook and Freddie Tilson transferred to the Manchester club from Barnsley. Outside left Brook put away 159 League and 19 FA Cup goals for his new team, while Tilson's tally was 110 League and 22 FA Cup goals.

Finishing third in Division One at the close of the 1929/30 season, City were knocked out of the FA Cup in Round Five, beaten 2-1 by Hull City.

Club record goal scorer Tommy Johnson moved to Everton in March 1930, for a £6,000 fee. Tommy had been with City since 1919, and ironically he appeared in the 1933

Everton squad when City lost 3-0 to the Merseysiders in the FA Cup Final.

On November 2nd, 1929 a certain Matt Busby played his City debut game against Middlesbrough. Matt was to make a significant contribution to Manchester football, later becoming manager of United. Not surprisingly, his life has been totally immersed in the game. In 1928, while representing a local club in Scotland, he was invited to join City.

The inside forward role for his new club did not suit the talented youngster, but injuries to other team mates meant that Matt played wing half in the reserves. The club quickly realised that this was his best position, and he soon acquired a regular first team place.

During 1929/30, Matt Busby turned out a dozen times for City in League and Cup games, scoring five goals. He featured in City's 1933 and 1934 Cup Finals and gained a Scotland cap against Wales in 1933. Three years after this, Matt went on to join Liverpool, becoming Manchester United's manager in 1946.

3

The 1930s and 1940s

The close of the 1930/31 season brought relegation for Manchester United, with City placed eighth in Division One. The meeting of the teams on October 4th, 1930 and on February 7th, 1931, resulted in impressive wins of 4-1 and 3-1 for the Maine Road club.

Personnel leaving Maine Road at the start of a new decade included director Lawrence Furniss and the famous Billy Austin. The latter was a gifted outside right who had come to Manchester from Norwich City in 1924. Turning out on 172 occasions for City in League and Cup matches, Austin had 47 goals to his credit. In 1931, he left Maine Road to try his fortunes with Chesterfield.

City finished sixteenth in the 1933 First Division at a time when the club boasted a strong defence. Langford was in nets, supported by the superb full backs Bill Dale and Syd Cann. Attacking prowess was provided by new signing Alec Herd who played his first League game for City against Blackpool in February 1933. He was to remain at Maine Road until 1948 when he transferred to Stockport County after representing City in almost 300 FA Cup and League Games.

FA Cup Success 1932-34

The early 1930s provided considerable F.A .Cup action for City fans as their team was placed fourteenth in the 1932 Division One table and sixteenth the following year.

Here is how the Maine Road side fared in the 1931/32 FA Cup competition:

Route to the 1932 FA Cup Semi-final

Date	Round	Opponents	Score
January 9th	Three	Millwall	3-2
January 23rd	Four	Brentford	6-1
February 13th	Five	Derby County	3-0
February 27th	Six	Bury	4-3
March 12th	Semi-final	Arsenal	0-1

1932 Semi-final

The City team was made up of:

Langford, Felton, Dale, Busby, Cowan, McMullan, Toseland, Marshall, Halliday, Tilson, Brook

The Blues dominated play for much of the game and things looked as though they were going City's way. Remarkably, in the last minute a shot from Arsenal's Bastin was punched away by City's goalie Langford, but the ball then hit the cross bar, shot back to the line, bounced off an upright and went into the net!

The crowd, Bastin, and of course Langford, were dumbfounded, but the score remained 1-0 and City were robbed of a Wembley Final success.

Manchester City

Bill Dale moved to City from arch-rivals United in 1931. Whilst with the Blues, this local lad gained a League Championship medal, FA Cup medal, and was a member of the 1933 Cup Final Squad. In this shot of City players training in the mid-1930s, we see (left to right), Heale, Brook, Barkas and Dale.

The 1933 Cup Final

This was the first of two consecutive Wembley appearances for the Maine Road club who were meeting Everton for the first time in an FA Cup tie.

The prelude to Wembley was full of drama, with Gateshead holding City to a 1-1 draw in an early round. In typical City fashion the North East club was demolished 9-0 in the replay! Subsequent victories were recorded against Walsall, Bolton Wanderers, Burnley and Derby County, as City kept up their momentum on the way to Wembley.

The team representing City on April 29th, 1933 against Everton at Wembley was:

Langford, Cann, Dale, Busby, Cowan, Bray, Toseland, Marshall, Herd, McMullan, Brook

City needed all the strength they could muster against Everton who were led by Dixie Dean. The Manchester fans feared the worst when Fred Tilson was left out of the squad. Injury forced the Blues' centre forward to relinquish his place on the team two weeks before the big match. He more than made up for this in 1934 when he scored the two vital goals which put an end to Portsmouth's chances in the F.A. Cup Final.

The 1933 Final was the first time that City had turned out in numbered shirts, and in order to avoid a colour clash with Everton, they sported a red and white strip.

A crowd of 93,000 waited for battle to commence at Wembley, and many City followers were curious to see how former Blues star Tommy Johnson would perform. As we have already seen he played with City from 1919-30, transferring to Everton for a £6,000 fee in March 1930. There were some rather anxious moments for City manager Wilf Wild who had succeeded Peter Hodge after his move to Leicester in 1932. The boss decided to leave out Tilson who had a leg injury, replacing him with Bobby Marshall who came in as inside right, while Herd moved to centre forward.

Route to the 1933 FA Cup Final

Date	Round	Opponents	Result	Scorers
Jan 14th	3	Gateshead	1-1	Toseland
Jan 18th	3 (Replay)	Gateshead	9-0	Tilson (3); Cowan (2); Busby; Barrass; McMullan; Brook
Jan 28th	4	Walsall	2-0	Brook (2)
Feb 18th	5	Bolton Wanderers	4-2	Brook (3); Tilson
March 4th	6	Burnley	1-0	Tilson
March 18th	Semi-final	Derby County	3-2	Toseland; Tilson; McMullan
April 29th	Final	Everton (at Wembley)	0-3	

There was no score until the fortieth minute when Stein beat Langford to make it 1-0 for Everton. During the first ten minutes of the second half, a tackle by Dean caused 'keeper Langford to drop the ball which found its way into the net. The third Merseyside goal came from Dunn, and City lost the FA Cup Final 3-0.

The fans were rather unhappy, and their spirits were not lifted when the team finished sixteenth in Division One.

1934, Wembley Again

The following year saw City on the Wembley trail once again at a time when they came a respectable fifth in the League. The success of 1934 attracted bumper crowds, with for example, 50,000 spectators watching the January Arsenal meeting when the Gunners went down 2-1.

The City faithful were hoping for great things from the club's new 'keeper Frank Swift. The Blues knocked out Blackburn Rovers, Hull City, Sheffield Wednesday, Stoke City and Aston Villa before taking on Portsmouth at Wembley in the 1934 F.A. Cup Final.

The home game with Stoke attracted a crowd of 84,569 which was one of the biggest to be recorded officially. This

Sam Cowan leads his team on to the hallowed Wembley turf for the 1934 FA Cup Final when City beat Portsmouth 2-1. The goal-scoring genius of Fred Tilson is perhaps best remembered in this game when he beat the Pompey 'keeper twice to help City to victory. Sam Cowan picked up the FA Cup from King George V after the exciting match. During his career with City, he played in three FA Cup Finals.

necessitated the gates being closed before the match started.

The previous record was in Round Four of the FA Cup on March 8th, 1924 when 76,166 people turned out to see a goalless draw against Cardiff City.

The obvious popularity of Manchester City was reflected in the large numbers of people who attended the various ties in the F.A.

Drama from the 1934 FA Cup Final when City defeated Portsmouth at Wembley in front of just under 94,000 spectators. The Blues looked sharp in this match where a 2-1 City victory was the outcome. To reach this prestigious Final, City beat Blackburn Rovers, Hull City, Sheffield Wednesday, Stoke City and Aston Villa. In this scene from the Wembley game, City have just launched an attack on the opposition, with 'keeper, Gilfillan trying to rebuff the Blues' advances.

Cup. For example, Round Five in February was enjoyed by 72,841 who witnessed a 2-2 draw with Sheffield Wednesday, while 68,614 went to the replay when City won 2-0.

City's Cup team enjoyed a leisurely break at Southport before travelling to Wembley. The team featured:

Swift, Barnett, Dale, Busby, Cowan, Bray, Toseland, Marshall, Tilson, Herd, Brook

There were only three changes in a side which had played at Wembley a year earlier, which consisted of:

Langford, Cann, Dale, Busby, Cowan, Bray, Toseland, Marshall, Herd, McMullan, Brook

Portsmouth scored first when Rutherford pounced on a pass from Weddle and blasted in a superb shot past Frank Swift. The score was 1-0 at half time, but in the second half, Tilson equalised. Following his run down the left wing, he sent the ball past Portsmouth's perplexed 'keeper, Gilfillan. Thanks to the ingenuity of Tilson who scored his second goal just three minutes from the end, City won 2-1. This was a worthy result for the Manchester club who were FA Cup winners for the first time since 1904.

Swift and Barkas

Significant acquisitions at this time were the legendary Frank Swift, the famous Sam Barkas and Jimmy Heale. Jimmy joined the Maine Road staff in January 1934 having moved from Bristol City. He remained with the Blues until his retirement in 1945.

Above: City star Jimmy Heale, seen here in action against Arsenal in the mid 1930s. Heale scored a total of 41 goals in 86 League and five FA Cup appearances for the Manchester club.

Moments to Remember

Vintage City in the mid-1930s when crowds of 30,000 to 40,000 were quite common. In this gripping encounter, Heale snatches a goal with his marvellous volley.

North Easterner Sam Barkas transferred from Bradford City in April 1934.

Captain of the Maine Road side when they clinched the Second Division Championship in 1946/7, Sam was a resilient and tenacious left back who made 195 appearances for City before assuming managerial duties at Workington in 1947. A decade later he returned to Maine Road where he acted as a scout for new talent.

Signing from Fleetwood in 1932, Frank Swift's first game for City was on Christmas Day 1933. Arguably one of soccer's most talented goalkeepers, "Big Swifty" was largely instrumental in City's winning the F.A. Cup in 1934, the League Championship for the first time in 1937, and the Second Division title ten years later.

Frank provided energy and inspiration, with his goalkeeping prowess being recognised at a national as well as local level. He won 19 England caps and represented City on 376 occasions.

"Swifty" gave up soccer in 1949 to follow a career in journalism, but sadly he died in the Munich air crash of 1958.

There was no repeat of the earlier FA Cup success in 1934/5 as City were beaten 1-0 by Spurs in Round Three.

The League performance, however, was quite impressive, City finishing a respectable fourth after a number of memorable games. The first two League fixtures in February 1935 saw them blast in 12 goals as they trounced Leicester 6-3 and Middlesbrough 6-2 in consecutive games. The new acquisition Heale made a significant contribution to City's success, scoring in ten League games during 1934/35.

League Champions, 1937

Sam Cowan left in 1935, and fans wondered if the club could find a suitable replacement. A year later, City sold Matt Busby to Liverpool for £8,000. The famous Scottish international had played in the 1933 and 1934 Cup Finals, representing City on 226 occasions and scoring 14 goals. Matt remained with Liverpool until World War Two, joining Manchester United as manager in 1946.

New personnel in the mid-1930s included Peter Doherty who came from Blackpool in June 1936 for a £10,000 fee. The clever Irish inside forward remained with City until 1945. The 1936/37 season was an unforgettable period as Doherty hammered home 32 goals, while colleague Eric Brook scored on 22 occasions in FA Cup and League games.

The close of the 1935/36 season brought ninth place for City in Division One, while Grimsby finished the club's hope of FA Cup success in Round Five.

1936/37 is a season emblazoned in the club's history as City won their first League Championship, finishing three points ahead of Charlton Athletic. They lost only one home match, 4-2 against Sunderland on October 31st, 1936.

City were in the lower half of the table until

Christmas 1936, but from this date they lost none of the remaining League games.

Some outstanding matches included the game against Manchester United in September 1936 when 69,000 saw Heale and Bray score as City went down 3-2. The Maine Road side made up for this on January 9th, 1937 as a crowd of almost 63,000 saw City beat the Reds 1-0.

Even more impressively, in March 1937, Liverpool were humbled by City in a 5-0 and a 5-1 defeat over a three day period.

As the closing games of the season loomed City awaited the results of each match with bated breath. This was at the time when Doherty headed home the club's 100th League goal, on April 17th when City beat Preston 5-2.

A week later, the Maine Road side needed just two points to clinch the League title. They achieved what the fans had been praying for. City ravaged Sheffield Wednesday 4-1 and then coasted to first place in Division One with a 2-2 draw at Birmingham. The regular squad in the 1936/37 Championship side comprised:

Swift, Percival, Herd, Dale,
Barkas (Captain), Doherty, Tilson,
Toseland, Bray, Marshall, Brook

Unfortunately this winning side did not remain intact for long with Fred Tilson, Billy Dale and Bobby Marshall leaving in 1938/39. Tilson's spell with City lasted from 1928-38, while Dale turned out on 269 occasions between 1931 and 1938. Marshall went to Stockport County in March 1939.

The League success more than compensated for the FA Cup defeat at the hands of Millwall in Round Six on March 6th, 1937.

Although City occupied the prime League spot at the close of the 1936/37 season, not all Manchester soccer fans were satisfied, as United were relegated to Division Two with Sheffield Wednesday.

Top of Division One 1936/37

	P	W	D	L	F	A	Pts
Manchester City	42	22	13	7	107	61	57
Charlton	42	21	12	9	58	49	54
Arsenal	42	18	16	8	80	49	52
Derby	42	21	7	14	96	90	49
Wolves	42	21	5	16	84	67	47
Brentford	42	18	10	14	82	78	46

Relegation, 1938

Les McDowall transferred from Sunderland for a £7,000 fee in 1938, becoming captain within 12 months of his arrival. In 1949, Les assumed managerial duties at Wrexham. He later managed the Blues between 1950 and 1963.

City were top of Division One in 1937, but the next year witnessed their relegation. Although the club was placed twenty-first in 1938 and were relegated, the faithful followers were full of high hopes at the start of Second Division soccer.

Before the first game of 1937/38, City

boasted an unbeaten run of 22 League games. However, the first match of the new season on August 28th, 1937, resulted in a 3-1 defeat at Wolves.

City's last match of the 1937/38 season kicked off with fans realising that their favourites were one of half a dozen clubs threatened by relegation. And so, on May 7th, 1938, they took on Huddersfield Town in front of 35,000 spectators when a win would have guaranteed City a Division One place.

Hopes were high, especially since they had performed well in front of some formidable opposition earlier in the season:

Date	Opponents	Score
September 18th 1937	Derby County	6-1
January 29th 1938	Derby County	7-1
April 16th 1938	West Bromwich Albion	7-1
April 30th 1938	Leeds United	6-2

Surely City could defeat Huddersfield Town. After all, they had amassed a staggering 80 goals – the highest number scored in Division One that season. But the Blues lost 1-0 and were relegated to Division Two with West Bromwich Albion.

Initially the prospects looked good at the outset of 1938/39 Division Two football, which opened with a 5-0 victory over Swansea followed by a 3-0 win against Chesterfield. City lost the next four games, going down 2-4 to both Bradford and West Ham. This was followed by a 2-1 win for Luton Town, and a 6-1 defeat by Millwall on September 17th, 1938.

However, the stoic fans did not let their team down, and on several occasions more than 30,000 people attended City's Second Division games. On November 19th, 1938 almost 39,000 witnessed City's 3-0 defeat of Coventry, while a game against Blackburn on January 28th attracted 45,400.

Part of the reason for City's popularity was the entertaining soccer produced by their players, including Herd, Doherty, Heale and Milsom. In 1938/39, the first two scored 20 and 17 League goals respectively, while Heale netted nine and Milsom 15.

In spite of this goal scoring ability, City could only manage two FA Cup ties. In a Round Three match with Norwich City, the they came out on top (5-0), but in the second tie, Sheffield United's 2-0 victory ended any Cup hopes they might have entertained.

The Second World War

Players and fans did their bit for the country in World War Two, with Frank Swift donning a Special Constable's uniform in Manchester.

Clearly, conscription reduced the number of spectators, but there were still some significant crowds at Maine Road games, the early war years sometimes witnessing gates of over 45,000. The local derby was still an attractive fixture, and when the Blues took on Manchester United in the League War Cup, more than 21,000 saw City win 1-0.

Moments to Remember

The City squad just before the outbreak of World War Two, with 'keeper Frank Swift standing head and shoulders above his colleagues. Normal soccer fixtures were scrapped during the hostilities, when City took part in the Western Regional League and the North Regional Section.

Following Germany's invasion of Poland in 1939, normal League games were suspended after just three matches in the season. These were superseded by regional football which brought City into contact with a number of clubs who would not normally share the same pitch.

City played in the North Regional League, and suffered some embarrassing defeats. For example, in January 1944, they only scored once in the 7-1 defeat by Bury when the Blues' goal was provided by Heale.

The match against Chester on December 16th, 1944 saw a similar score line when Bray supplied City's consolation goal. Here is how a typical Blues' squad looked in the Second World War period:

Chappell, Clark, Bray, Eastwood, Walsh, Bardsley, Barclay, Doherty, King, Chisholm, Leech

During the war years, City fans were able to see both Manchester clubs at the Maine Road ground. Neighbours United played

Manchester City

Examples of wartime fixtures

Date	Opponents	Result
May 4th 1940	Tranmere Rovers	2-1
May 18th 1940	Port Vale	7-0
December 14th 1940	Stockport County	9-1
November 20th 1943	Chester	2-1

there after Old Trafford had been severely damaged by bombs in 1941. The Reds paid a fee to City for the use of the stadium until their return to Old Trafford in August 1949.

Normal Soccer Once More

Once everything was back to normal after the War, City were desperate to regain Division One status. They had been in Division Two since 1938, just a season after winning the top Division Championship for

Sam and Mary Barkas about to enter the Kingsway Picture House at the junction of Moseley Road and Kingsway. Coming from Bradford City in 1934, Sam made 175 League and 20 FA Cup appearances for Manchester City before his move to Workington Town in May 1947.

the first time. The fans had every confidence in their team which featured a number of impressive players like Frank Swift, Sam Barkas, Les McDowall, Bert Sproston, Alec Herd and Andy Black. City performed well in the Division Two soccer League of 1946/47, enjoying a 3-0 win over Leicester in the opening match.

Prospects looked good with the Blues losing only twice in their first dozen League fixtures.

The period from November 16th, 1946 to April 19th, 1947 brought 22 League games without a single defeat. An impressive record by any standards.

Not surprisingly City were top of Division Two for the rest of the season, following the Fulham encounter on January 1st, 1947, in which the Londoners were humbled 4-0.

The promotion battle ended in May when the Maine Road side defeated Burnley by one goal in front of a 70,000 crowd. Now in top spot, City were guaranteed a First Division place the following year. However, this was a short-lived experience, since within three seasons they would be relegated for the fifth time.

Versatile Maine Road

City did not achieve much in the 1946/7 F.A. Cup competition, losing 5-0 to Birmingham City in Round Five. However, there were quite a few other things going on at the club to take the fans' minds off this.

Rivals Manchester United were still playing at City's ground as repairs went ahead at Old Trafford following the bomb damage. Further entertainment was also provided when the replayed Liverpool -v- Burnley F.A. Cup Semi-final was staged at Maine Road. The Rugby League Championship play-off between Wigan and Dewsbury was also held there on June 21st, 1947. A total of eleven such play-off Finals occurred at City's ground between 1938 and 1956, with the Maine Road club being quite delighted with their share of the gate receipts.

In November 1946, Sam Cowan took over managerial duties from Wilf Wild. The new boss had joined City as a player in 1924 following his transfer from Doncaster Rovers. Moving to Bradford City in 1935, Sam returned to Manchester as manager and guided City along the promotion path to Division One. Cowan was succeeded by Jock Thomson in 1947, mainly because Sam had a thriving physiotherapy practice in Brighton and did not want to give it up.

Players who came on the scene in the mid 1940s included the prolific scorer Andy Black. He transferred to Stockport County in 1949 after scoring 52 goals for City. Inside forward George Smith enjoyed his League debut for the Maine Road side on August

Top of Division Two 1946/47							
	P	W	D	L	F	A	Pts
Manchester City	42	26	10	6	78	35	62
Burnley	42	22	14	6	65	29	58
Birmingham	42	25	5	12	74	33	55

31st, 1946 when his new team took on Leicester City. Signing for the Blues in 1938, the striker served his country in the Second World War, and scored 80 goals between 1946 and 1952 before transferring to Chesterfield.

A couple of new wingers, Roy Clarke (Cardiff City) and Jack Wharton (Preston) wore the City strip for the first time in 1947. Welsh international Clarke proved his worth at Maine Road as a skilful left winger in 369 Cup and League games.

He was one of several City stars who moved to neighbours Stockport County, while Jack Wharton went to Blackburn in 1948.

An example of the City team at the close of the 1947 season is the side which faced West Ham in a Second Division League game on May 24th:

Thurlow, Sproston, Barkas, Fagan, McDowall, Emptage, Dunkley, Herd, Black, Smith, Westwood

City were 1-0 ahead at half time courtesy of a Les McDowall penalty, with George Smith volleying a thundering drive past 'keeper Ernie Gregory in the second half to make it 2-0.

The Blues' top position in Division Two at the close of the season assured promotion for 1947/48.

Back to Division One, 1947

City's new status in 1947/48 attracted big crowds at Maine Road, with 78,000 thronging the ground on September 28th to see a 0-0 draw in the Manchester derby.

City -v- United 1947-1953		
Date	City	United
1947/8	0	0
	1 (Linacre)	1 (Rowley)
1948/9	0	0
	0	0
1949/50	1 (Munro)	2 (Pearson, 2)
	1 (Black)	2 (Delaney; Pearson)
1951/2	1 (Hart)	2 (Berry; McShane)
	1 (McCourt)	1 (Carey)
1952/3	2 (Clarke; Broadis)	1 (Downie)
	1 (Broadis)	1 (Pearson)

In the return game in April 1948, almost 72,000 witnessed another draw, this time 1-1, goals coming from City's Linacre and United's Rowley. The first of these had arrived at Maine Road in 1947 from Chesterfield in part exchange for Tommy Capel. Linacre could float a ball across to the centre just as well as Finney or Matthews. City fans were therefore surprised when the outstanding star was allowed to move to Middlesbrough in 1949 at a time when the Ayresome Park club were in desperate need of a winger.

Linacre's goal against United in 1948 in the 1-1 draw is a reminder that there were quite a few low-scoring games between the Reds and the Blues in the next few years.

Manchester City

The FA Cup brought little success for City in 1947/8. They defeated Barnsley in Round Three, knocked out Chelsea in the subsequent round, but were eliminated from the competition 1-0 by Preston North End.

In the first home game of the 1948/49 season on August 25th, just seven seconds had elapsed when Preston North End's Bobby Langton stunned City with his early goal.

Happily, City and went on to win 3-2 with contributions by Sproston, McDowall and McMorran. Finishing seventh at the end of this season, City slumped to twenty-first position the following year, and were relegated.

The match against Bolton on November 6th, 1948. In this picture, a City defender wards off a Bolton attack in the game where Smith provided City's only goal. The final score was 5-1.

Moments to Remember

Maine Road action on April 2nd, 1949, when the home side beat Bolton Wanderers 1-0. City's goal came from Black, and the team eventually finished seventh in Division One.

4

The 1950s

Manager McDowall

1950 brought Division Two soccer for the Blues whose fans saw several people depart from Maine Road.

Manager Jock Thomson resigned after a two-year spell, and former player Les McDowall moved into the manager's chair during 1950. Remaining with the club for 13 years he introduced a number of innovations including the 'Revie Plan', which is described later.

McDowall's aim was to take City back into Division One, and this he accomplished during his first season.

Departures

Fans were concerned about the departure of three stars in this period. Frank Swift retired, Bert Sproston transferred to Ashton United in August 1950, while Andy Black moved to Stockport County the same month.

Frank Swift had kept goal for City since 1932 and had gained 19 England caps. Captaining his country in the international with Italy in 1948, 'Swifty' demonstrated some intriguing techniques. His accurate throws to wingers, for example, gave City forwards a head start over opposing defences.

This photograph shows Frank Swift receiving the Manchester Supporters' Club Presidency from Bill Miles.

Defender Bert Sproston had served City well as a dependable right back since 1938. He made one appearance for England while at Maine Road, to add to his 10 caps won at Leeds United and Tottenham Hotspur.

Andy Black was sadly missed by Maine Road crowds. This excellent goal scorer

Manchester City

Opposite: City occupied fifteenth place in Division One at the close of the 1951/52 season. In their good run up to January, they lost only seven out of 22 matches.

ravaged numerous opposition defences, scoring 15 goals in 1946/7 and 17 during the next season.

At the start of a new decade it is interesting to see the first team members. The 3rd Round of the FA Cup on January 7th, 1950 produced a typical line-up:

Powell, Phillips, Westwood, Gill, Fagan, Walsh, Oakes, Black, Turnbull, Alison, Clarke

No doubt this team wanted to put that particular FA Cup game behind them since they were eliminated by a Derby County 5-3 victory. City's goals were provided by Black (2) and Clarke.

1949/50

Sadly, City finished twenty-first out of 22 Division One teams at the close of the 1949/50 season, with only one away League victory against Sunderland in April 1950.

But, the Maine Road fans continued to rally round their team, with a 58,000 crowd attending the Blackpool game on September 24th when Stanley Matthews and his squad handed out a 3-0 defeat.

Not surprisingly the derby matches attracted large numbers. City faced the Reds on September 3rd and December 31st, 1949, going down to a hard-fought 2-1 on each occasion.

In September, Pearson supplied the United goals, while Munro provided City's consolation. It was Pearson in action once again in December when he and Delaney netted one each, while Black put City on the scoresheet. The attendances for these games were 47,705 and 63,704.

The League match against Derby on April 22nd, 1950 was crucial in terms of fighting off relegation, and almost 53,000 watched City draw 2-2. This put the Blues behind Charlton Athletic who still had a game in hand.

Charlton Athletic's victory over Derby in the League, coupled with City's 0-0 draw at West Bromwich Albion, meant relegation for the Manchester club, along with Birmingham.

In the 1949/50 season, City won only eight out of 42 League games. So for a season City entertained such teams as Doncaster Rovers, Grimsby Town and Brentford, before regaining a First Division place in 1951.

Bottom of Division One 1949/50

	P	W	D	L	F	A	Pts
Stoke	42	11	12	19	45	75	34
Charlton	42	13	6	23	53	65	32
Manchester City	42	8	13	21	36	68	29
Birmingham	42	7	14	21	31	67	28

Manchester City

		Arsenal	Aston Villa	Blackpool	Bolton Wanderers	Burnley	Charlton Athletic	Chelsea	Derby County	Fulham	Huddersfield T.	Liverpool	Manchester City	Manchester United	Middlesborough	Newcastle United	Portsmouth	Preston North End	Stoke City	Sunderland	Tottenham Hotspur	West Bromwich A.	Wolverhampton W.		
Arsenal	H	–	2-1	4-1	4-2	1-0	2-1	2-1	3-1	4-3	2-2	0-0	2-2	1-3	3-1	1-1	4-1	3-3	4-1	3-0	0-1	6-3	2-2	H	Arsenal
	A	–	0-1	0-0	1-2	1-0	3-1	3-1	2-1	1-0	0-3	2-2	0-0	2-0	1-6	3-0	0-2	1-1	0-2	1-2	1-4	2-1	1-3	1-2	A
Aston Villa	H	1-0	–	4-0	1-1	4-1	0-2	7-1	4-1	4-1	1-0	2-0	1-2	2-5	2-0	2-2	2-0	3-2	2-3	2-1	0-3	2-0	3-3	H	Aston Villa
	A	1-2	–	3-0	2-5	1-2	1-0	2-2	1-3	2-1	2-2	1-1	0-2	1-6	0-2	2-2	1-4	3-1	0-2	2-1	1-2	2-1	2-1	A
Blackpool	H	0-0	0-3	–	1-0	1-0	1-2	1-2	1-1	4-2	3-1	0-2	2-2	2-2	6-3	0-0	3-0	4-2	3-0	1-0	0-2	0-3	3-2	H	Blackpool
	A	1-4	0-4	–	0-1	1-0	0-2	0-2	1-2	1-1	1-2	3-1	1-1	0-0	1-3	0-1	3-1	3-1	1-3	3-2	3-1	0-0	0-3	A
Bolton Wanderers	H	2-1	5-2	1-0	–	1-4	2-1	3-0	1-2	2-2	2-1	1-1	1-2	1-1	2-1	1-0	3-1	0-0	0-3	1-1	1-1	1-1	3-2	2-2	H	Bolton Wanderers
	A	2-4	1-1	0-1	–	3-1	0-1	3-1	2-5	2-1	2-0	1-1	3-0	0-1	0-2	1-0	0-3	2-2	2-1	2-0	1-2	2-3	1-5	A
Burnley	H	0-1	2-1	2-0	1-3	–	1-0	1-1	0-1	1-0	0-2	0-0	0-0	1-1	7-1	2-1	1-0	0-2	4-0	0-1	1-1	6-1	2-2	H	Burnley
	A	0-1	1-4	0-1	4-1	–	0-1	1-4	0-2	1-1	3-1	1-3	1-6	0-5	1-7	2-2	2-1	1-2	0-0	1-1	1-1	2-1	A
Charlton Athletic	H	1-3	0-1	2-0	1-0	1-0	–	1-1	3-3	3-0	4-0	2-0	0-0	2-2	4-3	3-0	0-0	2-2	2-4	2-0	2-1	0-3	3-3	1-0	H	Charlton Athletic
	A	1-2	2-0	2-1	1-2	2-0	–	0-1	3-1	3-3	0-1	1-1	2-4	2-3	1-2	0-6	0-1	0-3	2-1	1-1	3-2	1-1	2-2	A
Chelsea	H	1-3	2-2	2-1	1-3	4-1	1-0	–	0-1	2-1	2-1	1-3	0-3	4-2	5-0	1-0	0-0	1-0	2-1	0-2	1-3	0-1	H	Chelsea
	A	1-2	1-7	2-1	0-3	1-1	1-1	–	1-1	2-1	1-1	1-3	0-3	0-0	1-3	0-1	0-1	1-2	1-1	4-2	2-3	1-0	3-5	A
Derby County	H	1-2	1-1	1-1	5-2	1-1	0-3	1-1	–	5-0	2-1	1-1	1-3	0-3	3-1	1-3	1-0	4-3	4-2	3-4	4-2	2-1	1-3	H	Derby County
	A	1-3	1-4	1-2	2-1	1-0	3-3	1-0	–	0-3	1-1	0-2	2-4	1-2	0-0	1-2	1-3	1-0	1-3	0-3	0-5	0-1	2-1	A
Fulham	H	0-0	2-2	1-2	1-2	1-2	3-3	1-2	3-0	–	1-0	1-1	1-2	3-3	6-0	1-1	2-3	2-3	5-0	0-1	1-2	1-0	2-2	H	Fulham
	A	3-4	1-4	2-4	1-2	0-1	0-3	1-2	0-5	–	0-1	0-4	1-1	2-3	0-2	1-0	0-4	1-0	1-1	2-2	0-1	2-0	2-2	A
Huddersfield T.	H	2-3	3-1	1-3	3-2	1-3	1-0	1-0	1-1	1-0	–	1-2	5-1	3-2	1-0	2-4	0-0	2-0	2-2	2-1	1-3	0-0	1-7	H	Huddersfield T.
	A	2-2	0-1	1-3	1-2	2-0	0-4	1-2	1-2	2-0	–	1-2	0-3	1-1	1-2	2-6	1-3	2-5	0-0	1-7	0-1	0-0	0-0	A
Liverpool	H	0-0	1-2	1-1	1-1	3-1	1-1	1-1	2-0	4-0	0-2	–	1-2	0-0	1-1	3-0	0-2	2-2	2-1	2-1	1-2	1-1	2-5	1-1	H	Liverpool
	A	0-0	0-2	0-2	1-1	0-0	0-2	3-1	1-1	1-1	2-1	–	2-1	0-4	3-3	1-1	3-1	0-4	2-1	1-0	0-3	3-2	3-3	1-2	A
Manchester City	H	0-2	2-2	0-0	0-3	0-1	4-2	3-1	4-2	1-1	3-0	1-2	–	1-2	2-1	1-2	2-3	0-1	1-0	0-1	3-1	1-1	1-2	0-0	H	Manchester City
	A	2-2	2-1	2-2	1-2	0-0	3-0	3-1	2-1	1-5	2-1	1-1	–	1-2	2-0	1-1	1-3	0-3	2-1	2-3	2-2	2-2	A
Manchester United	H	6-1	1-1	3-1	1-0	6-1	3-2	3-0	1-1	3-2	1-1	4-0	0-1	–	4-2	2-1	1-2	1-2	3-4	0-1	2-0	5-1	2-0	H	Manchester United
	A	3-1	5-2	2-2	0-1	1-1	2-2	2-4	3-0	3-3	2-3	0-0	2-1	–	4-1	2-2	1-0	0-2	1-0	0-2	3-3	2-0	A
Middlesborough	H	0-3	2-0	1-0	2-0	5-0	2-1	0-0	0-0	2-0	2-1	3-3	2-2	1-4	–	2-1	2-1	2-5	3-0	0-2	2-1	0-1	4-0	H	Middlesborough
	A	1-3	0-2	2-2	1-3	1-7	3-4	0-5	1-3	0-6	0-1	1-1	1-2	2-4	–	2-0	4-5	1-0	2-3	1-3	1-3	3-2	0-4	A
Newcastle United	H	2-0	6-1	1-3	0-1	7-1	6-0	3-1	2-1	0-1	6-2	1-1	1-1	0-2	0-2	–	3-3	3-0	6-0	2-2	7-2	1-4	3-1	H	Newcastle United
	A	1-1	2-2	3-6	0-0	1-2	0-3	1-3	1-1	4-2	0-3	3-2	1-2	1-2	–	1-3	2-2	1-5	4-4	1-1	2-3	3-3	0-3	A
Portsmouth	H	1-1	2-0	1-3	3-0	2-2	1-0	1-0	3-1	1-4	0-3	1-3	1-0	1-0	5-4	3-1	–	1-2	4-1	0-2	2-0	1-1	2-3	H	Portsmouth
	A	1-4	0-2	0-0	3-0	0-1	2-0	1-0	1-1	3-2	1-0	2-0	1-0	3-1	2-2	3-3	–	2-2	0-2	1-3	1-3	0-5	1-1	A
Preston North End	H	2-0	2-2	3-1	2-2	1-2	2-1	3-0	1-0	0-1	0-1	5-2	4-0	1-1	2-0	1-2	2-2	–	2-0	4-2	1-1	1-0	3-0	H	Preston North End
	A	3-3	2-3	3-0	1-1	2-2	4-0	3-4	3-2	0-2	2-1	5-2	0-3	2-1	1-1	0-0	0-0	–	0-1	1-1	1-4	2-1	A
Stoke City	H	2-1	4-1	2-3	1-2	2-1	1-2	1-1	2-1	1-1	0-0	3-2	4-5	2-0	0-0	–	1-1	1-6	1-1	1-0	H	Stoke City
	A	1-4	3-2	2-4	1-1	0-4	0-4	0-1	2-4	0-5	2-0	1-2	1-0	0-4	0-3	0-6	1-4	0-2	–	1-0	0-2	0-1	0-3	A
Sunderland	H	4-1	1-3	1-3	0-2	0-0	1-1	4-1	3-0	2-2	7-1	3-0	3-0	1-2	3-1	1-4	3-1	0-0	0-1	–	0-1	3-3	1-1	H	Sunderland
	A	0-3	1-2	0-3	1-1	1-0	1-2	1-2	4-3	1-0	2-2	2-2	1-3	1-0	2-0	2-2	2-0	2-4	1-1	–	0-2	1-1	3-0	A
Tottenham Hotspur	H	1-2	2-0	2-0	2-1	2-3	3-2	5-0	1-0	2-3	2-1	2-0	3-1	2-1	3-1	1-0	2-0	2-0	–	3-1	4-2	H	Tottenham Hotspur
	A	1-1	3-0	0-1	1-1	1-1	3-0	2-0	2-4	2-1	1-1	1-1	1-1	0-2	1-2	2-7	0-2	1-1	6-1	1-0	–	1-3	1-1	A
West Bromwich A.	H	3-1	1-2	1-1	3-2	1-1	1-1	1-0	1-0	0-2	0-0	3-3	3-2	3-3	2-3	3-3	5-0	1-1	0-1	3-1	–	2-1	H	West Bromwich A.
	A	3-6	0-2	0-2	2-3	1-6	3-3	3-1	1-2	0-1	0-6	5-2	2-1	1-5	1-0	4-1	1-0	0-1	1-1	3-3	1-3	–	4-1	A
Wolverhampton W.	H	2-1	1-2	3-0	5-1	1-2	2-2	5-3	1-2	2-2	0-1	2-2	0-2	4-0	3-0	1-1	1-4	3-0	0-3	1-1	1-4	–	H	Wolverhampton W.
	A	2-2	3-3	2-3	2-2	2-2	0-1	1-0	3-1	2-2	7-1	1-1	0-0	0-2	0-4	1-3	3-2	0-3	0-1	1-1	2-4	1-2	–	A

53

Bert Trautmann

Although disappointed at City's progress the fans could at least obtain some pleasure from new players. The most important acquisition at this time was the famous Bert Trautmann. Newcomers also included Bill Spurdle from Oldham and Blackburn's Dennis Westcott. This last player stayed at Maine Road for a couple of seasons while Spurdle remained until 1956.

Trautmann was a German paratrooper who was captured by the British, and then held in a Prisoner of War Camp in Northwich before being transferred to Ashton-in-Makerfield three years later. Following his release after the War, he worked on a farm and began playing football for St. Helens.

Signing for City in November 1949, Trautmann faced many problems. He had to take over from the legendary Frank Swift as goalkeeper, and it was not easy for a former German paratrooper to turn out before English crowds just a few years after hostilities had ceased.

But Bert soon won over the fans, playing in 545 League and Cup games including two FA Cup Finals. He was the first German to win a cup medal.

His cat-like qualities, daring and agility gave a tremendous boost to City as demonstrated in the important game with Division One leaders Sunderland on April 15th, 1950. Bert saved a penalty, and when the referee ordered it to be retaken, the talented 'keeper palmed it acrobatically to safety. The Manchester club eventually won 2-1 against a side which was to finish third in Division One.

City had only been in the premier League for three seasons before going down with Birmingham City in 1950. Large crowds still followed the Blues urging them on to regain Division One status.

This unstinting loyalty paid off as City were unbeaten in the first 10 League matches of the 1950/51 season.

They were top of Division Two in December 1950, and although the last three matches of the season resulted in draws, they were guaranteed promotion to Division One, finishing second, while Preston occupied the top slot.

Meadows, Revie and Leivers

In April 1950, Johnny Hannaway transferred from Seaforth, staying at Maine Road until he moved to Gillingham in 1957. There was sadness among the staff and fans in December 1950 when Wilf Wild died. He had acted as secretary-manager from 1932-46, and became secretary when Sam Cowan began his brief managerial spell in 1946.

The 1951/52 season included a number of new names on the team sheet such as Jimmy Gunning (from Hibernian), Jimmy Meadows, Roy Paul and Frank McCourt. The first of these represented the Blues from 1950-54 on 15 occasions before transferring to Barrow.

Bolton-born Jimmy Meadows came to City from Southport in 1951, but had his career

Manchester City

1952-53: a difficult season for City, hovering in the relegation zone of Division One.

55

Manchester City

curtailed following an injury in the 1955 Cup Final. He remained with City until his retirement in 1957. During his spell with the Blues, Meadows turned out 141 times in League and Cup matches, playing in several positions. He also gained one England cap, and later became trainer/coach for Manchester City, and then with Stockport County.

The early 1950s produced a few near misses in terms of relegation, as manager Les McDowall saw his team come fifteenth in 1951/2, twentieth the following season and seventeenth in 1953/4. The crowds were hoping for better things, particularly since their club had signed on some promising players including Don Revie from Hull and Sunderland's Ivor Broadis, both of whom came to Maine Road in October 1951.

In the period 1951-56 Don Revie scored 41 goals before departing for Sunderland, who parted with a £24,000 cheque. Don later became player-manager for a struggling Leeds. Ivor Broadis represented City between 1951 and 1953 as an inside forward, making over 70 appearances.

Bill Leivers' debut game was against Preston North End on August 21st, 1954. The stalwart's strong defensive skills saved City from many defeats in the 281 matches he played for the club. Transferring to Chesterfield in 1964, he later managed a number of sides including Cambridge United and Chelmsford City.

First Division final positions, 1952/53.

This is a significant table: City were battling to escape relegation when the last match saw them confront fellow-strugglers Chelsea. The Blues lost 3-1 but both clubs escaped relegation.

	P.	W.	D.	L.	F.	A.	W.	D.	L.	F.	A.	Pts.
Arsenal	42	15	3	3	60	30	6	9	6	37	34	54
Preston North End	42	15	3	3	46	25	6	9	6	39	35	54
Wolverhampton W.	42	13	3	5	54	27	6	8	7	32	36	51
W. Bromwich A.	42	13	3	5	35	19	8	5	8	31	41	50
Charlton Athletic	42	12	8	1	47	22	7	3	11	30	41	49
Burnley	42	11	6	4	36	20	7	6	8	31	32	48
Blackpool	42	13	5	3	45	22	6	4	11	26	48	47
Manchester Utd.	42	11	5	5	35	30	7	5	9	34	42	46
Sunderland	42	11	9	1	42	27	4	4	13	26	55	43
Tottenham Hotspur	42	11	6	4	55	37	4	5	12	23	32	41
Aston Villa	42	9	7	5	36	23	5	6	10	27	38	41
Cardiff City	42	7	8	6	32	17	7	4	10	22	29	40
Middlesbrough	42	12	5	4	46	27	2	6	13	24	50	39
Bolton Wanderers	42	9	4	8	39	35	6	5	10	22	34	39
Portsmouth	42	10	6	5	44	34	4	4	13	30	49	38
Newcastle Utd.	42	9	5	7	34	33	5	4	12	25	37	37
Liverpool	42	10	6	5	36	28	4	2	15	25	54	36
Sheffield Wednesday	42	8	6	7	35	32	4	5	12	27	40	35
Chelsea	42	10	4	7	35	24	2	7	12	21	42	35
Manchester City	42	12	2	7	45	28	2	5	14	27	59	35
Stoke City	42	10	4	7	35	26	2	6	13	18	40	34
Derby County	42	9	6	6	41	29	2	4	15	18	45	32

Achieving little in terms of League success, City did not provide much excitement for the fans in FA Cup matches between 1951 and 1954, as the club failed to go beyond Round Four.

Blues -v- Reds 1953/56

As the mid-1950s approached, prospects were improving for City who were seventh in Division One in 1955. This was mainly because the forwards could readily infiltrate the opposition's defences. Rivals City and United met in a number of confrontations between 1953 and 1956, with the Blues losing only one of the seven fixtures. One of these was an FA Cup tie in January 1955.

So who actually represented the two clubs in this era? As an example, look at the sides in the 1955 FA Cup tie on January 29th:

United: Wood, Foulkes, Byrne, Gibson, Chilton, Edwards, Berry, Blanchflower, Webster, Viollet, Rowsley

City: Trautmann, Meadows, Little, Barnes, Ewing, Paul, Fagan, Hayes, Revie, Hart, Clarke

City were certainly encouraged by the large crowds that turned out to support them: 57,663 people saw them beat West Bromwich Albion 4-0 in April 1955, while 60,000 saw Sunderland defeated 1-0 in the next League game.

City - v - Manchester United 1953-56

		Result		City Scorers
1953/54	**League** Sept. 5th	M/C Utd 0	M/C City 2	Revie; Hart
	Jan. 16th	M/C Utd 1	M/C City 1	McAdams
	League Sept. 25th	M/C Utd 2	M/C City 3	Fagan McAdams Hart
1954/55	Feb. 12th	M/C Utd 0	M/C City 5	Fagan(2) Hayes(2) Hart
	FA Cup (Round 4) Jan. 29th	M/C Utd 0	M/C City 2	Hayes Revie
	League Sept. 3rd	M/C Utd 0	M/C City 1	Hayes
1956/57	Dec. 31st	M/C Utd 2	M/C City 1	Dyson

Manchester City

The dependable and consistent Bert Trautmann is captured in action as he dives to keep out an opponent's effort at goal in 1953. The German 'keeper remained with the Blues from 1949-1964.

Manchester City

During his spell with City between 1951 and 1956, Don Revie put away 37 League goals. One of those occurred in this fixture with Bolton on October 23rd, 1954. The score of 2-2 was the result of the Burnden Park game when McAdams supplied City's second goal. In this fine piece of action some 40 years ago, a hard, low shot by Wheeler gives Bolton their first goal in the thrilling game played in front of 30,100 spectators.

The FA Cup Final 1955

In 1955, for the first time in over 20 years, City reached the Final of the FA Cup, by beating a number of leading teams, including their local rivals at Old Trafford.

City fans of the 1950s will vividly recall the tragedy which befell Jimmy Meadows in the 1955 Final against Newcastle United.

The 24-year old right full back damaged his right knee when he turned to tackle Newcastle's winger Bobby Mitchell. He was forced to leave the pitch, reducing the Blues to 10 men. Sadly, this tough defender had so badly damaged his knee ligaments that he never played again.

Both the club and fans were concerned about Jimmy's withdrawal since the Final squad already lacked Paul and Hart. Furthermore, 'keeper Trautmann was nursing shoulder and knee problems when he took to the pitch.

The City faithful hoped that the Revie Plan would lead to a victory. Introduced by manager McDowall, this strategy was named after Revie who wore the number nine shirt. It depended on a deep-lying centre forward, and was, in fact, based on the 1953 Hungarian system.

So the Final was under way. Unfortunately City were 1-0 down within the first minute, and a short time later Meadows was forced to quit.

Even though reduced to 10 men, City's heroic Bobby Johnstone headed home an equaliser from a Hayes' centre before half time. The second 45 minute spell brought two further goals from Newcastle, and so the final score read 3-1 in favour of the North East side.

This was the third F.A. Cup victory for Newcastle in a five year period, and was the first one involving City which had been shown on television.

1955/56: a good season for Manchester soccer

What a memorable time for City fans. The Blues were at Wembley again in 1956 as Manchester's soccer fraternity were agog with excitement. In that year, City won the F.A. Cup, and United topped the League in Division One. The Maine Road club was fourth, three positions higher than in 1955.

Although this was one of the most enjoyable years in the history of Manchester football, some City fans were disappointed. Before the 1955/6 season started Revie had been transfer listed, and he played most of his games in the Reserves.

Route to the 1955 FA Cup Final

Round	Club	Result	Scorers
3	Derby County	3-1	Barnes; Hayes; Revie
4	Manchester United	2-0	Hayes; Revie
5	Luton Town	2-0	Clarke (2)
6	Birmingham City	1-0	Hart
Semi final	Sunderland	1-0	Clarke
Final	Newcastle United	1-3	Johnstone

Manchester City

Wembley Again!

In order to reach Wembley, City had to defeat Blackpool, Southend, Liverpool, Everton and Tottenham. The team endured some awful weather conditions, with the Blackpool game of January 7th, 1956 having to be abandoned because of a blanket of fog. In the replay the following week the teams battled on through a muddy Maine Road pitch when the home side won 2-1.

Following a 0-0 draw against Liverpool on February 18th, City went to a snow-laden Anfield where the Blues won 2-1.

It was certainly a tough F.A. Cup run for both players and fans who braved the inclement weather. But there was considerable excitement too. In the Round Six match against Everton for example, City were 1-0 down at half time. However, in the sixty-eighth minute Hayes nodded in a free kick to level the score at 1-1. Johnstone's superb seventy-sixth minute header found the back of the net, and the final score read Everton 1, Manchester City 2.

It was the stylish Johnstone who pulled it out of the bag for City a couple of weeks later in the fortieth minute of the Semi-final with Tottenham. He executed a magnificent flying header following a Clarke centre. The 90 minute score of 1-0 took City through to Wembley largely thanks to Johnstone's inspired display and the admirable team composure.

FA Cup Final 1956

Cup Finals are remembered for a number of reasons. There was the over-the-line goal of 1932, the Matthews Final in 1953, and the resistance displayed by Arsenal when reduced to 10 men in 1952.

And the match of May 5th, 1956 should be included in these Great Finals. Some would refer to it as the Revie Final, because of the major role he exerted on the game. The Manchester players went to Wembley with Roy Paul as the captain of a side which included Ken Barnes. This last player had secured a regular first team place from 1954, having joined the club from Stafford Rangers. Don Revie replaced Billy Spurdle who was suffering from boils on the eve of the big match.

Here is the 1956 Cup Final team, eight of whom had been to Wembley the previous year:

Trautmann, Leivers, Little, Barnes, Ewing, Paul, Johnstone, Hayes, Revie, Dyson, Clarke

The Manchester players kept the ball on the ground, and demonstrated a laid-back way of play. They built up the attacks in an almost lazy manner, and Birmingham were perplexed by this Hungarian-style play.

In the third minute Revie delivered a 40 yard drive to Clarke on the left wing. Yelling for a return pass, Don tricked the defence, and pushed the ball to Joe Hayes whose splendid left foot volley made it 1-0 for City.

Moments to Remember

Dubbed "The Revie Final", the Wembley fixture of 1956 gave City a well-deserved 3-1 victory over Birmingham. Revie was included in the Manchester team only on the morning of the match when Spurdle was declared unfit.

Opposite: City came fourth in Division One of the 1955/56 season, playing 42 League games and losing only 14. One of the few upsets was an early-season 7-2 defeat by Wolves on August 27th. City went on to overcome most of the opposition.

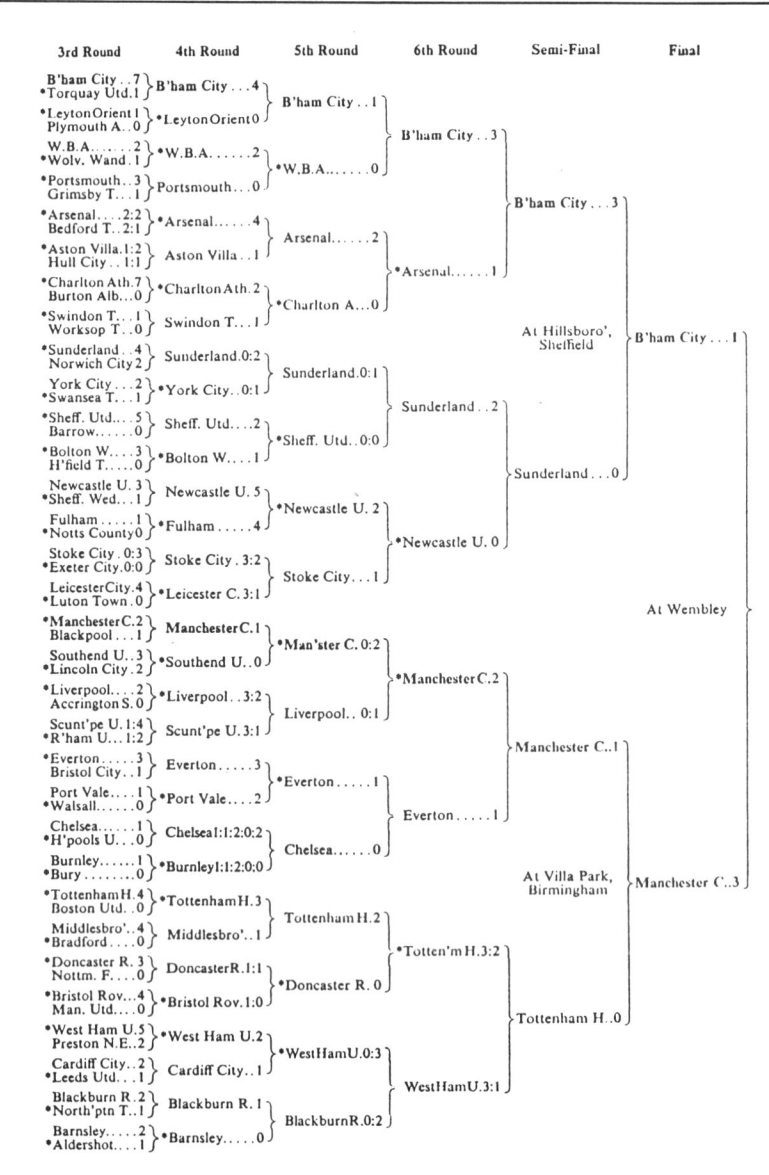

3rd Round	4th Round	5th Round	6th Round	Semi-Final	Final
B'ham City..7 / *Torquay Utd.1	B'ham City...4	B'ham City..1	B'ham City..3	B'ham City...3	B'ham City...1
LeytonOrient 1 / Plymouth A..0	*LeytonOrient 0				
W.B.A.....2 / *Wolv. Wand..1	*W.B.A......2	*W.B.A......0			
*Portsmouth..3 / Grimsby T...1	Portsmouth...0				
*Arsenal....2:2 / Bedford T..2:1	*Arsenal......4	Arsenal......2	*Arsenal......1		
*Aston Villa.1:2 / Hull City..1:1	Aston Villa..1				
*Charlton Ath.7 / Burton Alb..0	*Charlton Ath.2	*Charlton A...0			
Swindon T...1 / Worksop T..0	Swindon T...1			At Hillsboro', Sheffield	
*Sunderland..4 / Norwich City 2	Sunderland.0:2	Sunderland.0:1	Sunderland..2		
York City...2 / Swansea T...1	*York City..0:1				
*Sheff. Utd...5 / Barrow......0	Sheff. Utd....2	*Sheff. Utd...0:0		Sunderland...0	
Bolton W...3 / H'field T....0	*Bolton W.....1				
Newcastle U. 3 / *Sheff. Wed...1	Newcastle U. 5	*Newcastle U. 2	*Newcastle U. 0		
Fulham......1 / Notts County 0	*Fulham......4				
Stoke City..0:3 / *Exeter City.0:0	Stoke City..3:2	Stoke City...1			
LeicesterCity.4 / *Luton Town..0	*Leicester C. 3:1				
*Manchester C.2 / Blackpool...1	Manchester C.1	*Man'ster C. 0:2	*Manchester C.2	Manchester C..1	Manchester C..3
Southend U..3 / *Lincoln City.2	*Southend U..0				
*Liverpool....2 / Accrington S. 0	*Liverpool...3:2	Liverpool...0:1			
Scunt'pe U. 1:4 / *R'ham U...1:2	Scunt'pe U. 3:1				
*Everton.....3 / Bristol City..1	Everton.....3	*Everton......1	Everton......1		
Port Vale....1 / *Walsall......0	*Port Vale....2				At Wembley
Chelsea......1 / *H'pools U...0	Chelsea 1:1:2:0:2	Chelsea......0			
Burnley......1 / *Bury........0	*Burnley 1:1:2:0:0				
*Tottenham H.4 / Boston Utd..0	*Tottenham H.3	Tottenham H.2	*Totten'm H.3:2		
Middlesbro'..4 / *Bradford....0	Middlesbro'..1			At Villa Park, Birmingham	
*Doncaster R. 3 / Nottm. F....0	Doncaster R. 1:1	*Doncaster R. 0			
*Bristol Rov...4 / Man. Utd....0	*Bristol Rov.1:0			Tottenham H..0	
*West Ham U.5 / Preston N.E..2	*West Ham U.2	*West Ham U.0:3			
Cardiff City..2 / *Leeds Utd...1	Cardiff City..1		West Ham U.3:1		
Blackburn R..2 / *North'ptn T..1	Blackburn R. 1	Blackburn R.0:2			
Barnsley.....2 / *Aldershot....1	*Barnsley.....0				

* Home Club in first match

Manchester City

		Arsenal	Aston Villa	Birmingham City	Blackpool	Bolton Wanderers	Burnley	Cardiff City	Charlton Athletic	Chelsea	Everton	Huddersfield T.	Luton T.	Manchester City	Manchester United	Newcastle United	Portsmouth	Preston North End	Sheffield United	Sunderland	Tottenham Hotspur	West Bromwich A.	Wolverhampton W.	
Arsenal	H	–	1-0	1-0	4-1	3-1	0-1	3-1	2-4	1-1	3-2	2-0	3-0	0-0	1-1	1-0	1-3	3-2	2-1	3-1	0-1	2-0	2-2	H Arsenal
	A	–	1-1	0-4	1-3	1-4	1-0	2-1	1-0	2-1	1-1	0-2	2-5	1-0	2-0	1-3	1-3	1-2	3-3	A
Aston Villa	H	1-1	–	0-0	1-1	0-2	2-0	2-0	1-1	1-4	2-0	3-0	1-0	0-3	4-4	3-0	1-3	3-2	3-2	1-4	0-2	3-0	0-0	H Aston Villa
	A	0-1	–	2-2	0-6	0-1	0-2	0-1	1-3	0-0	1-2	1-1	1-2	2-2	0-1	3-2	2-2	1-0	2-2	1-5	3-4	0-1	0-0	A
Birmingham City	H	4-0	2-2	–	1-2	5-2	1-2	2-1	4-0	3-0	6-2	5-0	0-0	4-3	2-2	3-1	3-2	0-3	0-2	1-2	3-0	2-0	0-0	H Birmingham City
	A	0-1	0-0	–	0-2	0-6	2-3	1-2	0-2	2-1	1-5	1-1	1-0	1-1	1-2	2-2	5-0	1-1	3-0	0-1	1-0	2-0	0-1	A
Blackpool	H	3-1	6-0	2-0	–	0-0	1-2	1-5	2-0	4-0	4-2	3-2	2-0	1-0	0-0	5-1	2-3	2-6	1-1	7-3	0-2	5-1	2-1	H Blackpool
	A	1-4	1-1	2-1	–	3-1	2-0	0-1	2-1	1-2	0-1	1-3	1-3	0-2	1-2	2-1	3-3	3-3	1-2	0-0	1-1	2-1	3-2	A
Bolton Wanderers	H	4-1	1-0	6-0	1-3	–	0-1	4-0	1-3	4-0	1-1	2-2	4-0	1-3	3-1	3-2	4-0	0-0	2-1	0-3	3-2	4-0	2-1	H Bolton Wanderers
	A	1-3	2-0	2-5	0-0	–	0-2	0-1	1-3	2-0	0-1	1-3	0-0	0-2	0-1	0-3	3-3	1-0	3-1	0-0	3-0	0-2	2-4	A
Burnley	H	0-1	2-0	3-2	0-2	2-0	–	0-2	2-1	5-0	0-1	2-0	3-1	2-2	0-0	3-1	3-0	1-2	1-1	4-0	2-0	1-2	1-2	H Burnley
	A	1-0	0-2	2-1	1-1	1-0	–	2-2	1-2	0-0	1-1	0-1	3-2	2-1	0-3	1-1	3-3	2-4	2-1	4-4	1-0	0-1	1-3	A
Cardiff City	H	1-2	1-0	2-1	1-0	1-0	0-2	–	3-1	1-1	3-1	1-2	2-0	4-1	0-1	1-1	2-3	3-1	3-2	3-1	0-0	1-3	1-9	H Cardiff City
	A	1-3	0-2	1-2	1-2	0-4	2-0	–	0-0	1-2	0-2	2-1	0-3	1-3	1-1	0-4	1-2	1-2	1-1	1-1	1-1	1-2	2-0	A
Charlton Athletic	H	2-0	3-1	2-0	1-2	3-1	2-1	0-0	–	1-2	0-2	4-1	2-2	5-2	3-0	0-2	6-1	2-1	3-2	2-1	1-2	5-1	0-2	H Charlton Athletic
	A	4-2	1-1	0-4	0-5	3-1	1-2	1-3	–	1-3	2-3	0-4	1-2	2-0	1-5	1-4	0-4	2-2	0-0	2-3	3-2	3-3	0-2	A
Chelsea	H	2-0	0-0	1-2	2-1	0-2	0-0	2-1	3-1	–	6-1	0-0	0-2	2-1	2-4	2-1	1-5	0-1	1-0	2-3	2-0	2-1	2-3	H Chelsea
	A	1-1	4-1	0-3	1-2	0-4	0-5	1-1	2-1	–	3-3	3-1	2-2	2-2	0-3	1-1	4-4	3-2	1-2	3-4	0-4	0-3	1-2	A
Everton	H	1-1	2-1	5-1	1-0	1-0	1-1	2-0	3-2	3-3	–	5-2	0-1	1-1	4-2	0-0	0-2	0-4	1-4	1-2	2-1	2-0	2-1	H Everton
	A	2-3	0-2	2-6	0-4	1-1	1-0	1-3	2-0	1-6	–	0-1	2-2	0-3	1-2	2-1	0-1	0-1	0-1	0-0	1-1	0-2	0-1	A
Huddersfield T.	H	0-1	1-1	1-3	1-1	3-1	1-0	1-2	2-4	0-1	1-3	–	0-2	3-3	0-2	2-6	1-0	0-2	1-2	4-0	1-0	1-0	1-3	H Huddersfield T.
	A	0-2	0-3	0-5	2-4	2-2	0-2	2-1	1-4	0-0	2-5	–	2-1	0-1	0-3	1-1	1-2	5-1	1-3	1-4	2-1	2-1	0-4	A
Luton T.	H	0-0	2-1	0-1	3-1	1-0	0-2	3-0	2-1	1-2	2-2	1-2	–	3-2	0-2	4-2	1-1	2-1	8-2	2-1	1-0	2-1	5-1	H Luton T.
	A	0-3	0-1	0-0	2-3	0-4	1-3	0-2	2-2	0-0	1-0	2-0	–	2-3	1-3	0-4	0-0	1-2	4-0	2-1	1-2	1-3	2-1	A Luton T.
Manchester City	H	2-2	2-2	1-1	2-0	2-0	1-3	3-1	0-2	2-2	3-0	1-0	3-2	–	1-0	1-2	4-1	0-2	3-1	4-2	1-2	2-0	2-2	H Manchester City
	A	0-0	3-0	3-4	1-0	3-1	2-2	1-4	2-5	1-2	1-1	3-3	2-3	–	1-2	1-3	4-2	3-0	1-1	3-0	1-2	4-0	2-7	A Manchester City
Manchester United	H	1-1	1-0	2-1	2-1	1-0	2-0	1-1	5-1	3-0	2-1	3-0	3-2	5-2	–	5-2	1-0	3-2	3-1	2-1	2-2	3-1	4-3	H Manchester United
	A	1-1	4-4	2-2	0-0	1-3	0-0	1-0	0-3	4-2	2-4	2-0	2-0	0-1	–	0-0	2-3	1-3	0-1	2-2	2-1	4-1	2-0	A
Newcastle United	H	2-0	2-3	2-2	1-2	3-0	0-3	1-4	4-0	4-1	1-1	1-2	1-1	4-0	3-1	–	2-1	5-0	4-2	3-1	1-2	0-3	3-1	H Newcastle United
	A	0-1	0-3	1-3	1-5	2-3	1-3	1-1	1-2	0-1	2-0	1-2	0-0	6-2	2-4	–	2-0	3-4	1-2	6-1	1-3	1-1	1-2	A
Portsmouth	H	5-2	2-2	0-5	3-3	3-3	3-1	1-1	4-0	4-4	1-0	5-2	0-0	2-4	3-2	0-2	–	0-2	1-1	2-1	4-1	1-1	2-1	H Portsmouth
	A	3-1	3-1	2-3	3-2	0-4	0-3	3-2	1-6	5-1	2-0	0-1	1-4	0-1	1-2	1-2	–	1-2	3-1	2-4	1-1	0-4	1-3	A
Preston North End	H	0-1	0-1	1-1	3-3	0-1	4-2	1-2	2-2	2-3	0-1	1-2	1-2	0-3	3-1	4-3	2-1	–	0-2	2-2	3-3	0-1	2-0	H Preston North End
	A	2-3	2-3	3-0	6-2	0-0	2-1	1-3	2-1	2-1	4-0	2-2	1-2	2-0	2-3	0-5	2-0	–	1-3	2-2	4-0	2-3	1-2	A
Sheffield United	H	0-2	2-2	0-3	2-1	1-1	1-3	1-2	2-1	1-0	0-2	1-1	3-1	0-4	1-1	1-0	2-1	1-3	–	2-3	2-0	2-2	3-3	H Sheffield United
	A	1-2	2-3	2-0	1-1	1-2	1-1	2-3	2-2	2-3	0-1	4-1	2-1	1-2	1-3	3-2	4-1	1-2	–	2-3	1-3	1-2	2-3	A
Sunderland	H	3-1	5-1	1-0	0-0	0-0	4-4	1-1	3-2	4-3	0-0	4-1	1-2	0-3	2-2	1-6	4-2	2-2	3-2	–	3-2	2-1	1-1	H Sunderland
	A	1-3	4-1	2-1	3-7	3-0	0-4	1-3	1-2	3-2	2-1	0-4	2-8	2-4	1-2	1-3	2-1	2-2	3-2	–	3-2	0-3	2-3	A
Tottenham Hotspur	H	3-1	4-3	0-1	1-1	0-3	0-1	1-1	2-3	4-0	1-1	1-2	2-1	2-1	1-2	3-1	1-1	0-4	3-1	2-3	–	4-1	2-1	H Tottenham Hotspur
	A	1-0	2-0	0-3	2-0	2-3	0-2	0-0	2-1	0-2	1-2	0-1	2-1	2-2	2-1	1-4	3-3	0-2	2-3	–	0-1	1-5	A
West Bromwich A	H	2-1	1-0	0-2	2-1	2-2	1-0	2-1	3-3	3-0	2-0	1-2	3-0	1-0	4-1	4-1	1-0	3-2	2-1	3-0	1-0	–	1-1	H West Bromwich A
	A	0-2	0-3	0-2	1-5	0-4	2-1	3-1	1-5	5-0	2-0	0-2	1-3	3-0	1-1	1-0	2-2	1-2	1-4	–	2-3	A
Wolverhampton W	H	3-3	0-0	1-0	2-3	4-2	3-1	1-0	2-0	2-1	1-0	4-0	1-2	7-2	0-2	2-1	3-1	2-1	3-2	3-1	5-1	3-2	–	H Wolverhampton W
	A	2-2	0-0	0-0	1-0	2-3	1-2	2-1	9-1	2-0	3-2	1-2	3-1	1-5	2-2	3-4	1-3	1-2	0-2	3-3	1-1	1-2	1-1	–	A Wolverhampton W

63

A Kinsey equaliser produced a half-time score of 1-1 but in the second period the Blues scored a couple of incredible goals in just two minutes!

Revie's inspirational role once more assisted in the first goal, as Dyson scored. Then Johnstone's contribution made it a convincing 3-1 victory for the Blues. This was the score by which they had lost in the previous Final against Newcastle in 1955.

Of course the 1956 Wembley game with Birmingham will be remembered for Bert Trautmann's bravery. He valiantly played the last quarter of an hour with a broken neck!

Just 14 minutes from the final whistle Bert made a sensational dive at the feet of Birmingham's Murphy. He collided with the opponent, and the subsequent injuries required lengthy treatment from City's trainer. In spite of the terrific pain, the 'keeper persevered until the end of the game, and it was only after the final whistle that the break was discovered.

The fans were delighted with the 1956 victory, especially since City were the first club to play in the FA Cup Final at Wembley in successive seasons – not only in 1933 and 1934, but also in 1955 and 1956.

1957 FA Cup

In 1956/57 City slumped to eighteenth place, but the following season saw with City coming a respectable fifth. In 1957/58, the Blues scored 104 goals and had 100 put past them – phenomenal statistics when compared to other clubs.

Top of Division One 1957/58	
	Pts
Wolves	64
Preston	59
Tottenham	51
West Bromwich	50
Manchester City	49
Burnley	47
Blackpool	44
Luton	44
Manchester United	43

Some fans were disappointed that Don Revie did not make many first team appearances in 1956/57. The massive Jack Savage was in nets at the start of the season. The 6ft 4ins gentle giant had been signed in 1953 from Halifax Town, and was goalie until Bert Trautmann had recovered fully from the Cup Final injury.

One particularly dramatic match in this period was the replay of the Third Round of the FA Cup on January 9th, 1957 against Newcastle United.

Cup-holders City had drawn 1-1 with the Tynesiders four days earlier, but in the replay they were 3-0 up in the first 25 minutes. They maintained this lead until the end of an invigorating first half, and the supporters were quite confident that City would make it to the next round.

However, a couple of Newcastle goals after the break brought the fans to the edge of their seats. The 85th minute saw Curry head the equaliser.

The match moved into extra time when Johnstone made it 4-3 for the Blues in the seventh minute.

Once again, Newcastle moved in with a White goal to bring the scores level at 4-4. The same player then pounced on a Mitchell pass to put City out of the Cup. So the Blues lost 5-4, even though they had been 3-0 up within the first half hour.

Almost Relegation

There was considerable sadness in Manchester following the Munich air disaster in which former City star Frank Swift perished along with several United players.

The close of the 1950s saw City struggling again to retain their First Division place. Positioned twentieth in 1958/59 they confused the critics with their performances.

One of the many entertaining games was played against Portsmouth on March 7th, when the Blues were 2-0 down at half time. Suddenly, they produced four goals in an eight minute period, the final score reading 4-3.

Of course people wondered if the Blues could make a similar impression in the closing games of 1959 when relegation was just around the corner.

The vital match was with Leicester City on April 29th. Almost 47,000 spectators crushed into Maine Road knowing that Portsmouth would drop down to Division Two next season, along with either City or Aston Villa. This last team was playing West Bromwich Albion.

At half time, the City -v- Leicester score read 1-1, but eventually the home side came out on top, 3-1.

Suddenly the final score of the other crucial game was flashed to the Maine Road crowd who were ecstatic on discovering that Villa had lost.

In 1959/60, City played 42 League games of which they won 17, including a 3-0 defeat of Manchester United on September 19th. The Blues finished sixteenth while Burnley were in the premier position.

	P.	W.	D.	L.	F.	A.	W.	D.	L.	F.	A.	F.	A.	Pts
Burnley	42	15	2	4	52	28	9	5	7	33	33	85	61	55
Wolverhampton Wand.	42	15	3	3	63	28	9	3	9	43	39	106	67	54
Tottenham Hotspur	42	10	6	5	43	24	11	5	5	43	26	86	50	53
West Bromwich Albion	42	12	4	5	48	25	7	7	7	35	32	83	57	49
Sheffield Wednesday	42	12	7	2	48	20	7	4	10	32	39	80	59	49
Bolton Wanderers	42	12	5	4	37	27	8	3	10	22	24	59	51	48
Manchester United	42	13	3	5	53	30	6	4	11	49	50	102	80	45
Newcastle United	42	10	5	6	42	32	8	3	10	40	46	82	78	44
Preston North End	42	10	6	5	43	34	6	6	9	36	42	79	76	44
Fulham	42	12	4	5	42	28	5	6	10	31	52	73	80	44
Blackpool	42	9	6	6	32	32	6	4	11	27	39	59	71	40
Leicester City	42	8	6	7	38	32	5	7	9	28	43	66	75	39
Arsenal	42	9	5	7	39	38	6	4	11	29	42	68	80	39
West Ham United	42	12	3	6	47	33	4	3	14	28	58	75	91	38
Everton	42	13	3	5	50	20	0	8	13	23	58	73	78	37
Manchester City	42	11	2	8	47	34	6	1	14	31	50	78	84	37
Blackburn Rovers	42	12	3	6	38	29	4	2	15	22	41	60	70	37
Chelsea	42	7	5	9	44	50	7	4	10	32	41	76	91	37
Birmingham City	42	9	5	7	37	36	4	5	12	26	44	63	80	36
Nottingham Forest	42	8	6	7	30	28	5	3	13	20	46	50	74	35
Leeds United	42	7	5	9	37	46	5	5	11	28	46	65	92	34
Luton Town	42	6	5	10	25	29	3	7	11	25	44	50	73	30

Moments to Remember

City had to struggle to keep out of the relegation zone in 1959/60. A noteworthy game was the Wolves match on September 5th, 1959, when almost 44,000 saw ten goals scored.

5

The 1960s

League Upsets 1960-64

Maine Road crowds saw their team placed fifteenth, thirteenth, twelfth and eventually twenty-first in Division One between 1960 and 1963.

Towards the end of March 1961, a goalless draw against Bolton put the Maine Road team just two points clear of the bottom club. The next League game was with Preston North End who were also trying to avoid relegation. City lost 3-2, before being beaten 1-0 by Wolves, completing 1960/61 season in thirteenth place. The next year saw them one position higher, while in 1962/63 they were twenty-first in Division One. This meant Second Division soccer in 1963/64 with the Blues in sixth position, followed by eleventh slot the next year. But top place in 1965/66 took City back into Division One.

The League Cup and FA Cup 1960-65

The Cup competitions provided a respite from the difficulties the Blues were experiencing in the First Division, and their best performance was reaching the League Cup Semi-final in 1963/64.

City produced some outstanding football as they took on a variety of clubs.

If one were to single out a memorable match in the F.A. Cup competition, it would be the 6-2 win against Luton Town. City's new signing, the predatory Denis Law, ruthlessly exposed the Luton defence in that encounter before it was abandoned. He also scored City's consolation goal, when the tie was replayed.

Route to the League Cup Semi-Final 1963/64

Round	Date	Opposition	Score
2	Sept.25th	Carlisle Utd	2-0
3	Oct.16th	Hull City	3-0
4	Nov.27th	Leeds Ltd	3-1
5	Dec.17th	Notts.County	1-0
Semi-final (First Leg)	Jan.15th	Stoke City	0-2
Semi-final (Second Leg)	Feb.5th	Stoke City	1-0 (Agg.1-2)

FA Cup matches 1960-1965

Year	Round	Opponents	Result	Scorer
1960/1	3	Cardiff City	1-1	Opp. own goal
	3(Replay)	Cardiff City	0-0	
	3(Second replay)	Cardiff City	2-0	Law; Hayes
	4	Luton Town (abandoned)	6-2	Law (6)
	4	Luton Town	1-3	Law
1961/2	3	Notts. County	1-0	Young
	4	Everton	0-2	
1962/3	3	Walsall	1-0	Harley
	4	Bury	1-0	Harley
	5	Norwich City	1-2	Oakes
1963/4	3	Swindon Town	1-2	Oakes
1964/5	3	Shrewsbury Town	1-1	Kevan
	3(Replay)	Shrewsbury Town	1-3	Gray

Law, Young, Pardoe and Oakes

City parted company with Les McDowall in 1963 following his 13 years as manager. Assistant George Poyser took over the reins until the arrival in 1965 of the famous Joe Mercer.

In 1959/60, winger Andy Kerr transferred from Partick Thistle. The following season saw Jackie Plenderleith arrive from Hibernian, while another close season signing, Barrie Betts, came from Stockport County in June 1960.

In 1961/62 Peter Dobing (Blackburn) and Bobby Kennedy (Kilmarnock) arrived on the scene. Glyn Pardoe was an amateur on City's books from 1961 before turning professional two years later.

The immensely talented Neil Young signed up as a professional in February 1961 after being an apprentice at Maine Road. This was also the year when 17 year old David Wagstaffe was introduced to the squad.

Perhaps the most important acquisition in 1960 was Denis Law who arrived in March following City's paying £56,000 for Huddersfield Town's inside forward.

Before looking at the new players in detail, here is a typical side which took part in Round Three of the F.A. Cup against Cardiff City on January 7th, 1961, when the score was 1-1:

Trautmann, Leivers, Betts, Barnes, Plenderleith, Shawcross, Barlow, Law, Hannah, Hayes, Sambrook.

Denis Law

The Aberdeen-born player moved to Huddersfield where he made his League debut at just under 17 years of age in the game against Notts County.

The flamboyant striker played his first League game for City on March 19th, 1960 against Leeds United. Denis soon made his mark with the fans and management at Maine Road, scoring on 23 occasions in League and FA Cup games during 1960/61.

Denis felt the urge to try his hand on the continent, moving to the Italian side Torino for £125,000 in July 1961. There, he played alongside Joe Baker who had been with the Scottish club Hibernian. The Italian media gave the duo a rough time, and Denis's problems were compounded by the fact that at one stage, Torino would not allow him to play for his native Scotland.

A year or so after moving to Italy, Denis signed for Manchester United. The Reds paid Torino a record fee of £100,000 for the talented Scot.

Interestingly, this superlative striker made the short trip across Manchester in 1973 to rejoin the Maine Road club. He scored his last goal in League soccer in April 1974, when his infamous back-heel relegated Manchester United after the exciting derby in which the Reds lost 1-0.

Neil Young

The impressive local lad from Fallowfield signed as an apprentice player with City in 1959, becoming a full time professional during February 1961.

Although a proven left winger, Neil had to contend with Ray Sambrook, Clive Colbridge and David Wagstaffe, all of whom were vying for a coveted position on the squad.

Young's League debut for City was against Aston Villa in November 1961, when he played outside right at the tender age of 17.

The dependable and consistent forward-stayed with City until 1972 when he was sold to Preston North End. Neil had entertained thousands of Maine Road fans over the years, acquiring medals for the League Championship, European Cup Winners' Cup and the FA Cup.

Glyn Pardoe and Alan Oakes

What a colossus Glyn Pardoe turned out to be, experiencing 14 playing seasons during City's heyday of the late 60s and 70s.

He came to Maine Road in 1961, three years after his cousin, Alan Oakes, donned the City shirt. The unstinting loyalty displayed by the duo is quite apparent on considering their lengths of service with the Blues.

Oakes played a staggering 669 games between 1958 and 1976, accumulating a large number of medals. He then signed for Chester, as player-manager.

The first of Pardoe's 376 appearances for the Maine Road club was in a League game against Birmingham City in April 1962.

Both United and City fans were saddened by the events of a derby in 1970 when Glyn broke a leg. Following his recovery, he made a number of appearances in League games before retiring in April 1976. Perhaps he is best remembered for his winning goal in the 1970 League Cup Final at Wembley.

Barnes and Ewing Go

People moving to pastures new in the early 1960s included Ken Barnes and Dave Ewing.

The steadfast Barnes had arrived in 1950 from Stafford Rangers, and waited almost one and a half years for his first League game against Derby County in 1952. The determined and dedicated wing half remained with the Blues for a decade before becoming Wrexham's player-manager.

The father of one-time City winger Peter Barnes then returned to Maine Road as Chief Scout in 1974.

He began the 1991/92 season as Youth Development Officer with Terry Farrell, and his devotion to the club was rewarded by a testimonial at the end of that season.

Defender Dave Ewing was the backbone of City in the 1950s. Coming to Maine Road in June 1949 from Luncarty Juniors, the tough Scot had to wait until January 3rd, 1953 for his initial League game against Manchester United when a 1-1 draw ensued.

This fiery centre-half represented the Blues on 302 occasions until his departure for Crewe Alexandra in 1962. He later rejoined City as a coach, moved away, and came back to run the Reserves in the late 1970s.

Mercer and Allison

Les McDowall occupied the manager's chair in the 1950-63 period, followed by George Poyser who carried on until 1965. The mid 1960s looked grim for Manchester City, with the manager resigning in a season when the club finished eleventh in Division Two.

Help was on hand however, as the Joe Mercer era dawned at Maine Road. Under his leadership City became Division Two Champions for the sixth time when in 1965/6 they lost only five League games.

Fans hoped that Joe would bring a bit of stability to the club, since before his arrival there had been several personnel changes at Maine Road. Ten players had been allowed to go on free transfers, while manager George Poyser and trainer Jimmy Meadows resigned in 1965. Bert Trautmann left in 1963, while Joe Hayes departed the following year.

Arriving at Maine Road in 1965, the former manager of Sheffield United and Aston Villa had played wing half for Everton, Arsenal and England. Joe gained five international caps, and like Matt Busby, he became a member of the Army's Physical Training Corps when World War Two broke out.

Mercer's liaison with right hand man Malcolm Allison seemed to work and the club prospered. However, in 1972 he decided to try his fortunes with Coventry City as general manager, later becoming director of the club. Following Sir Alf Ramsey's departure in 1974, Mercer became caretaker manager of the England squad. This unassuming man from Ellesmere Port lived on the Wirral until his death on August 9th, 1990.

Just before the start of the 1965/66 season, Mercer invited 37 year old Malcolm Allison to join the Maine Road staff. The flamboyant personality had at one stage been centre half for West Ham, and then went on to manage Southern League side Bath City. Following his spell with Plymouth Argyle this top class coach teamed up with Joe Mercer.

The soccer world wondered if this partnership would last. The chemistry seemed to work as City almost immediately won the Second Division Championship in 1965/6 losing only five out of 42 matches. Promotion was guaranteed when Bell scored his goal in the 1-0 victory over Rotherham on May 4th, 1966. Below shows how City finished their spell in Division Two.

Top of Division Two 1965/66	
	Pts
Manchester City	59
Southampton	54
Coventry	53
Huddersfield	51
Bristol City	51
Wolves	50

The Mercer-Allison combination was later to be instrumental in gaining the Division One League Championship in 1968 (when United came second); the FA Cup in 1969 and also the League Cup, plus the European Cup Winners' Cup in 1970.

Allison's tactical skills coupled with Mercer's paternal approach provided not only good results, but also attractive soccer full of prolonged attacking play.

The City faithful were not to know that the thriving partnership would wane. Joe left in August 1972, leaving Malcolm to take over the reins. He stayed at Maine Road for only eight months before tendering his resignation.

In the early rounds of the 1965/66 FA Cup competition City knocked out Blackpool, Grimsby and Leicester.

Three matches then followed with Everton who eventually eliminated City from the Cup 2-0.

The Blues had already faced Leicester City in the League Cup competition earlier that season, when the Manchester side defeated them 3-1 in Round Two. An unfortunate own goal by Alan Oakes in the next Round allowed Coventry to push City out of the League Cup (3-2).

Heslop, Summerbee, Bell and Book

When it came to the acquisition of new players, Mercer and Allison took the bull by the horns, buying Colin Bell for £45,000 from Bury, and paying out £35,000 to Swindon for Mike Summerbee. The latter played his first League game for the Blues on August 21st, 1965 against Middlesbrough, while Bell's initial outing occurred on March 19th, 1966.

The former Everton centre-half George Heslop played his first League game for City in September 1965, the dependable defender contributing much to the club between 1965 and 1972.

City were in a state of flux in the mid-1960s with a number of departures which included Joe Hayes. Moving to Barnsley in 1966 after 13 years at Maine Road, this slightly built player took part in two FA Cup Finals and represented the Blues in 331 League games.

FA Cup 1965/66

Round	Date	Opposition	Score
3	Jan 22nd	Blackpool	1-1
3 Replay	Jan 24th	Blackpool	3-1
4	Feb 12th	Grimsby Town	2-0
5	March 5th	Leicester City	2-2
5 Replay	March 9th	Leicester City	1-0
6	March 26th	Everton	0-0
6 Replay	March 29th	Everton	0-0
6 Second Replay	April 4th	Everton	0-2

To give an idea of a typical City side in the mid-1960s we can look at the team which drew 0-0 in Round Six of the FA Cup tie replay with Everton on March 26th 1966:

Dowd, Kennedy, Horne, Doyle, Heslop, Oakes, Connor, Crossan, Summerbee, Young, Pardoe

Now a detailed look at four major acquisitions in 1965/66 – Heslop, Summerbee, Bell and Book.

George Heslop

Playing his first City game in September 1965, the Wallsend-born centre half acquired several medals at Maine Road before transferring to Bury in 1972.

He later became landlord of the Hyde Road Hotel Ardwick which was adjacent to City's (or Ardwick's) ground when the club played in that district between 1897 and 1923. This one-time Chester's pub was the scene of many interesting soccer conversations in those early years when it also served as the main office for the football club.

Mike Summerbee

Moving from Swindon Town to Maine Road in 1965, Mike was a tenacious winger, who also made a number of appearances at centre forward.

The crowds were delighted with the stylish Summerbee whose League debut against Middlesbrough was on August 21st, 1965.

Mike's name first appeared on the score sheets when the Blues secured a consolation goal in a 3-1 defeat by Birmingham on December 4th, 1965.

Summerbee went on to make a positive contribution to City's success, scoring 67 goals between 1965 and 1975 in League and Cup games.

In the mid-1960s, Sir Alf Ramsey was looking closely at City personnel, and he eventually chose seven Maine Road players to represent England. The first to receive this honour was Mike Summerbee whose initial England outing was in an under-23 game with Turkey.

The Swinging Sixties scene in Manchester saw Mike and United's George Best making quite an impression off the field as well as on it.

Mike moved to Burnley in 1975, and following a brief stint at Blackpool became player-manager for Stockport County.

Colin Bell

The very reasonable fee of £45,000 paid to Bury now seems a meagre amount considering how much Bell was to flourish at local and international level.

Playing his first full game for City in March 1966, this young man was full of drive and energy. Colin demonstrated several important attributes including anticipation, awareness and speed. It was a pleasure to watch him harass opposing defences with his boundless energy and unnerving body swerves.

Colin Bell had a pronounced effect on City's

destiny in the mid-1960s, scoring on his debut against Derby County and developing into the archetypal modern midfield player.

Remaining at Maine Road until injury forced him to play his final game in 1979, Bell made almost 500 appearances for City in a variety of League games and other competitions. He was another Blues star who represented England. Scoring 152 goals for City, he boasted a cabinet full of trophies and medals including awards for the F.A. Cup, League Cup, League Championship and the European Cup Winners' Cup.

Colin still maintains his affiliation with Maine Road, where he is involved with coaching the various youth teams.

Tony Book

In 1966, Tony Book first appeared on the team sheets. The close-season signing was 31, but age proved to be no problem for someone with such a wealth of experience.

This loyal man has been associated with Maine Road for almost a quarter of a century. Who can forget the contributions made by this £17,000 signing from Malcolm Allison's old club, Plymouth Argyle?

A star player of the later 1960s and early 1970s, Tony was captain when the Blues won the 1967/68 First Division title, the European Cup Winners' Cup, F.A. Cup and the League Cup.

The orthodox defender remained on the playing staff until 1973/74 when he became assistant to Ron Saunders, acting as manager in his own right in the 1974-79 period. Tony later assumed Reserve Team Coach duties, and today he is the First Team Coach.

Many a young player of the 1990s could do worse than study his loyalty, tenacity and professional approach to soccer demonstrated over the years.

City reach Round Six of 1967 F.A. Cup

In a season when Tony Coleman signed for the Blues, the F.A. Cup competition saw City go as far as Round Six, having earlier beaten Leicester City, Cardiff City and Ipswich Town. Games with the last two sides necessitated replays.

In Round Six, Leeds United dashed any hopes City had of reaching Wembley, when a controversial Jack Charlton goal gave the Yorkshire side a 0-1 victory on April 8th 1967.

In the League Cup, Bolton were defeated 3-1 in Round Two at Maine Road, but West Bromwich Albion knocked out City 4-2 in the next stage of this competition.

1967/68: Reds and Blues go for the League

This was a memorable season as City and United vied for the League Championship.

Soccer mania gripped Manchester as the Reds marched towards that First Division title. City fans were very concerned, since a confident United had not lost a single

League game between November 11th and February 3rd, 1968.

Needless to say, the derby matches of this period proved most exciting as both clubs aimed for the same championship title. Opposite is what happened on the two League encounters.

In the second of these confrontations City were a goal down after 35 seconds, but Colin Bell provided the equaliser.

George Heslop then scored his first League goal for City, and Lee's penalty made it 3-1. No doubt 'keeper Ken Mulhearn can bring to mind his tough debut in the September derby, when he replaced Harry Dowd who had broken a finger in a warming-up session.

City drew with Liverpool in the first game on August 19th, 1967, losing the next couple of matches to Southampton and then Stoke.

Book missed a penalty in the Liverpool game. In the match with Newcastle in September, Neil Young also shot wide from the spot.

Francis Lee's appearance clearly affected City's progress. He played his initial match against Wolves on October 14th, 1967, and from then until Boxing Day, the Blues were unbeaten in eleven League games. Lee's career will be considered later.

By Christmas, City were occupying a comfortable place in Division One, and during 1968 continued to achieve considerable

City -v- United 1967/68

Date	Result		Scorers
Sept 30th	City	1	Bell
	United	2	Charlton (2)
March 27th	United	1	Best
	City	3	Bell; Heslop; Lee

success, their first defeat of the year occurring on March 23rd when Leeds won 2-0.

Following their beating of Everton on April 29th, 1968, City had topped the table with just two League matches remaining. They moved nearer the elusive title with a convincing 3-1 win over Spurs on May 4th, and just one game remained. This was the meeting with Newcastle United.

The tension before this crucial meeting was unbearable particularly since a few weeks earlier it had looked as though the trophy would stay at Old Trafford. United were top of Division One in 1966/67, and in the following season they were five points ahead of their rivals at one stage, and so seemed to be in a strong position.

As it happened, the North East had a pronounced effect on the outcome of the 1968 Championship. United's last game was at home to Sunderland who had just escaped relegation worries under new boss Alan Brown, while City were away to Newcastle on May 11th, 1968.

So, as the game with the North Easteners kicked off the question was: "Could City bring home the League Championship to Maine Road for the second time in the club's history?"

In a crowd of 46,000, some 19,000 had travelled North from Manchester to cheer on the Blues.

First, Summerbee scored just 19 minutes into the game, while Bryan Robson put Newcastle on level pegging two minutes later. Neil Young made it 2-1 for the Blues, and once more the North East side levelled, this time courtesy of a Sinclair goal.

Another Neil Young contribution gave the Blues a 3-2 advantage, and then Francis Lee added his name to the list of scorers. Could City pull it off? A few minutes from the end, a Newcastle effort produced the final score-line of 4-3 for the Manchester side.

And Manchester United? They lost 2-1 to Sunderland, and as a consequence, City won the Championship by two points.

Top of Division One 1967/68

	P	W	D	L	F	A	Pts
Manchester City	42	26	6	10	86	43	58
Manchester United	42	24	8	10	89	55	56
Liverpool	42	22	11	9	71	40	55
Leeds	42	22	9	11	71	41	53
Everton	42	23	6	13	67	40	52
Chelsea	42	18	12	12	62	68	48

Francis Lee

Hailing from Westhoughton, Lancashire, the bubbling Francis Lee represented Bolton Wanderers with whom he made his debut as a 16 year old in 1960/61.

Moving to Maine Road in 1967, this stylish player soon won the affection of the crowds. A born entertainer, the dynamic Francis remained with City until his transfer to Derby County in 1974. In his 320 games for the Blues he unleashed many devastating volleys against confused 'keepers which led to a tally of 143 goals.

Who can forget his successful 1971/72 season when he scored thirty-three League goals, one League Cup goal and another in the F.A. Cup?

'Franny' is remembered for so much. On a light-hearted note, he earned the nickname Lee One Pen on account of his abilities to score from penalties with such apparent ease.

It was the game with Newcastle at St. James' Park, a year or so after Lee joined City, which changed his soccer career. Sir Alf Ramsey had journeyed to the North East to watch the game, and a few weeks later Francis was picked to represent England against Bulgaria.

Clearly, a player of Lee's calibre amassed a large number of trophies and awards while at Maine Road. These included winners' medals for the F.A. Cup and League Cup, together with those for winning the League Championship and the European Cup Winners' Cup.

Moving to Derby County in 1974, Francis acquired another championship medal while at the Baseball Ground. Capped 27 times for England, this Cheshire-based entrepreneur retired from soccer in 1976 to concentrate on his highly successful business ventures.

1969 FA Cup

Things were going well for City in the 1969 and 1970 seasons. In the next two seasons they would win the Charity Shield, F.A. Cup, League Cup, and European Cup Winners' Cup.

City successes 1968-1970	
1968	- Football League Division One Champions
	- FA Charity Shield Winners
1969	FA Cup - Winners
1970	European Cup Winners' Cup - Winners
1970	Football League Cup - Winners

What a season 1968/69 turned out to be as Tony Book was nominated joint Footballer of the Year, along with Derby's Dave Mackay. Newcomers to Maine Road, Arthur Mann from Hearts (£65,000) and Bobby Owen from Bury (£35,000) must have felt proud to belong to such a successful club. Although finishing thirteenth in Division One of 1969, City prospered well in the F.A. Cup, going on to face Leicester City in the Final.

Route to the Final

Mike Summerbee did not play in the Luton match where a Lee penalty provided the only goal in a somewhat pedestrian game. In the Semi-final, credit must go to teenager Tommy Booth who scored the crucial goal in the closing moments of the match. The game was climaxed by the delightful left foot shot which took the Blues to Wembley.

Wembley at Last!

The F.A. Cup Final was played on March 26th when City defeated Leicester 1-0.

This epic event at Wembley was the fourth season on the run that Leicester and City had come face to face in an F.A. Cup tie.

The Maine Road squad comprised:

Dowd, Book, Pardoe, Doyle, Booth, Oakes, Summerbee, Bell, Lee, Young, Coleman

The breakthrough in the game finally came when the long-striding City forward, Young, drilled a well-aimed volley into the roof of the net.

Neil's goal was the culmination of a move initiated by Summerbee who tricked David Nish, and pushed the ball past Leicester's Woollett. Young ran forward and blasted in a left foot drive past Peter Shilton, the Leicester and England Under-23 goalie. City fans were delirious and felt it would have been a gross injustice if their team had not won this game. The F.A. Cup was on its way back to Maine Road for the first time in 13 years.

Manchester City

Route to the 1969 FA Cup Final				
Date	Round	Opponents	Result	Scorers
Jan 4th	Three	Luton Town	1-0	Lee
Jan 25th	Four	Newcastle United	0-0	
Jan 29th	Four (Replay)	Newcastle United	2-0	Owen; Young
Feb 24th	Five	Blackburn Rovers	4-1	Lee (2) Coleman (2)
Mar 1st	Six	Tottenham	1-0	Lee
Mar 22nd	Semi-final	Everton	1-0	Booth
Apr 26th	Final	Leicester	1-0	Young

Next page: Joe Corrigan in action. He joined the club in 1966 and remained until 1983. With 476 League appearances to his credit, Joe put in 37 F.A. Cup and 52 League Cup games.

European Soccer

August saw City thrash West Bromwich Albion 6-1 in the F.A. Charity Shield, with goals courtesy of Lee (2), Owen (2), Young and an own goal by the opposition.

The Manchester club faced Huddersfield Town and Blackpool in the League Cup, the latter knocking City out of the competition (1-0) on September 25th, 1968.

City's League title success meant they were allowed to play in the European Cup for the first time. In the initial leg of the preliminary round the Blues drew 0-0 with Turkish champions Fenerbahce on September 18th, 1968. The second leg was held at the National Stadium in Istanbul, when City gave up a one goal lead, allowing Fenerbahce to win 2-1. The only City goal was scored by Coleman, and the Blues were sent packing from the European Cup competition with an aggregate score of 1-2. The squad in both games comprised:

Mulhearn, Kennedy, Pardoe, Heslop, Doyle, Oakes, Lee, Bell, Summerbee, Young, Coleman

A bit of consolation for dejected City followers was that the strong Turkish side had conceded only 12 goals in 34 matches.

Many fans questioned why their team could not have performed better, considering that the squad was practically the same as the one which had won the League title the previous season, and was clearly a force to be reckoned with.

City did not spend vast amounts of money on new players in the late sixties, when many were interested in how Joe Corrigan's career was progressing.

Joining the Blues as a junior in 1966 he waited until March 11th, 1969 to play his first League game against Ipswich Town. The highly-rated goalkeeper proved to be a valuable member of the City squad, enjoying almost 600 games for the Blues before moving to a North American club in 1983.

Considered by many to be one of the three top 'keepers in England, Joe represented his country on several occasions.

Manchester City

6

The 1970s

Manchester Clubs in Cup Games

The Manchester derby games provided the usual tension and excitement, but can you imagine the atmosphere among fans when a two-leg Semi-final in the Football League and an FA Cup round both involved City and United?

The road to the Football League Cup started in September when Southport and then Liverpool were knocked out by City with results of 3-0 and 3-2.

In the tie with Everton, goals by Bell and Lee guaranteed City a place in Round Five after they beat the Merseysiders 2-0.

The next team to give way was Queens Park Rangers (3-0), with Bell (2) and Summerbee doing the necessary at Maine Road. One of the London club's players was Rodney Marsh, who was to leave Q.P.R. in March 1972 to play for City.

City -v- United 1969/70

	Results	Scorers
League Games		
November 15th	City – 4	Bell (2); Young; opposition o.g.
	United – 0	
March 28th	City – 2	Lee; Doyle
	United – 1	Kidd
FA Cup		
(Round Four)		
January 24th	City – 0	
	United – 3	Kidd (2); Morgan
League Cup		
December 3rd	City – 2	Bell; Lee
(Semi-final, First Leg)	United – 1	Charlton
December 17th		
(Semi-final, Second Leg)	City – 2	Summerbee; Bowyer
	United – 2	Edwards; Law

(City won 4-3 on aggregate)

The two-leg Semi-final against Manchester United opened with a Maine Road meeting on December 3rd, 1969. The home side dominated the first half, going into the changing room at half time 1-0 up, thanks to Colin Bell.

Bobby Charlton provided the equaliser, but a penalty awarded in the last couple of minutes gave City a 2-1 victory. Fans looked forward to the Semi-final return game at Old Trafford on December 17th.

The 63,418 crowd saw Bowyer open the scoring but goals from Edwards and Law made it 2-1 for United on the night and 3-3 on aggregate.

As the minutes ticked by, extra time seemed likely but then fate took a hand. City were awarded an indirect free kick on the edge of the Reds' penalty area and Francis Lee thundered a direct shot at goal. Amazingly, 'keeper Stepney parried the shot, but only straight to Mike Summerbee who scored the goal which took the team to Wembley.

Remember, it was an indirect free kick, but in the tension of the derby, Alex Stepney turned a harmless shot into City's passport to the League Cup Final on March 7th.

The Blues had just returned from a European Cup Winners' Cup match with the Portuguese side Académica Coimbra on March 4th. Exhausted from their exploits abroad, City turned out on a muddy pitch at Wembley in bitterly cold conditions.

Here is the team that played against a West Bromwich side which inculded Asa Hartford who was to transfer to City in August 1974:

Corrigan, Book, Mann, Doyle, Booth, Oakes, Heslop, Bell, Summerbee, Lee, Pardoe, Bowyer (sub)

Jeff Astle gave Albion a sixth minute lead and an hour elapsed before Mike Doyle's equaliser.

With no further goals in normal time, Glyn Pardoe emerged the match winner as his shot beat Osborne in the West Bromwich goal after twelve minutes of extra time.

This allowed City to land the League Cup in the first season all ninety-two League clubs had taken part in the competition.

City's superb 2-1 victory meant the Blues were to become the first English club to win a major European and domestic trophy in one season.

Into Europe

European Cup Winners' Cup

City were in Europe once more, and just had to improve on their performance against Fenerbahce the previous season. This they did in no uncertain manner. They snatched up the Cup Winners' Cup in 1970 and reached the Semi-final the following year.

City battled on through the various rounds to pick up the prestigious trophy following a 2-1 victory on a rain-soaked Vienna night. And the Blues deserved to win.

No matter which club you followed, there was considerable interest shown about this time in the Cup Winners' Cup. City were

Moments to Remember

Route to the European Cup Winners' Cup

Round	Opponents	Result	Scorers
One (First Leg)	Atletico Bilbao (a)	3-3	Booth; Young; opp. o.g.
One (2nd Leg)	Atletico Bilbao (h)	3-0 (Agg. 6-3)	Bowyer; Bell; Oakes
Two (First Leg)	S.K. Lierse (a)	3-0	Lee (2); Bell
Two (2nd Leg)	S.K. Lierse (h)	5-0 (Agg. 8-0)	Bell (2); Lee (2); Summerbee
Three (First Leg)	Académica Coimbra (a)	0-0	
Three (2nd Leg)	Académica Coimbra (h)	1-0 (Agg. 1-0)	Towers
Semi-final (First Leg)	Schalke 04 (a)	0-1	
Semi-final (2nd Leg)	Schalke 04 (h)	5-1 (Agg. 5-2)	Young (2); Bell; Lee; Doyle
Final	Gornik Zabrze (In Vienna)	2-1	Lee; Young

experiencing a number of problems which attracted sympathy. For example, Joe Corrigan valiantly turned out with a broken nose when the German side Schalke 04 came to Maine Road. Injury prevented Bell and Heslop from taking part in the return leg against the Portuguese Club Académica Coimbra. Nevertheless, City persevered and reached the Final.

The match took place in Vienna on a wet April 29th 1970 against the Polish side Gornik Zabrze. Neil Young and Francis Lee supplied the goals for the 2-1 victory and 'Lee One Pen' appeared in press reports, reminding us of how Franny could convert a spot kick to a goal.

A small crowd of 12,000 attended the Final where it took City just twelve minutes for Neil Young put his side ahead. With half time approaching, he was fouled, and it was then that Lee blasted in the penalty.

The Poles scored in the sixty-eighth minute, but City remained on top – and there it was! The European Cup Winners' Cup was on its way to Maine Road.

In only five seasons, the renowned Mercer-Allison combination had guided City to five trophies: the League Championship, League Cup, European Cup Winners' Cup, Second Division Championship and the FA Cup. City were determined to keep the prestigious European trophy. The prospects looked good in the 1970/1 run up to the Cup Winners' Cup as the Blues crushed Linfield, Honved, and (once again) Gornik Zabrze.

Sadly, City gave in to Chelsea in the second leg of the Semi-final when the aggregate score read 2-0 for the Londoners.

The U.E.F.A. Cup

In 1972/3, the Blues had a short-lived run in the U.E.F.A. Cup:

The U.E.F.A. Cup 1972/3

Round	Opponents	Result	Scorers
One (First Leg)	Valencia (h)	2-2	Mellor; Marsh
One (Second Leg)	Valencia (a)	1-2	Marsh

(City lost 4-3 on aggregate)

The Domestic Scene 1970/72

We have already referred to the electric atmosphere surrounding the clashes between City and United in 1969/70. The Blues were tenth in Division One at the close of that season, going on to win the League Cup against West Bromwich (2-1) on March 7th 1970, after meeting United in the two Semi-finals.

Dowd Leaves

Local lad and former plumber Harry Dowd was born in 1938. Taking over from Bert Trautmann in nets, he played an important role in City's return to Division One soccer in 1965/6. He is one of the few 'keepers to actually score a goal. This was on February 8th 1964 when City drew 1-1 with Bury. Dowd left Maine Road for Oldham Athletic in December 1970.

Finishing eleventh in Division One 1971, City won only 12 out of 42 games.

The team did not score in 17 of the League games played during 1970/71.

Injuries did not help this situation, with Booth and Oakes nursing cartilage problems. Again, there was, of course, Glyn Pardoe who suffered a fractured leg following a tackle in the Manchester derby of December 12th, 1970. To aggravate the situation, one end of the stadium was closed all season for rebuilding.

Perhaps some enjoyment for the Maine Road faithful came in the form of a convincing 4-1 victory over United in that game. Francis Lee scored a memorable hat-trick, while Doyle added the finishing touch.

The FA Cup, 1971

Non-League Wigan Athletic arrived at Maine Road on January 2nd, 1971, to take on the First Division side in Round Three of the F.A. Cup.

City's hopes were high, but it was only a last-minute Colin Bell goal that saved the Blues the embarrassment of a replay at Wigan.

Following the 1-0 result, a 3-0 thrashing of Chelsea enabled City to reach Round Five. In this encounter with Arsenal, the London side's Charlie George produced two fine goals, with City's consolation effort coming from Colin Bell.

New Players

Two new faces at this time included Willie Donachie and Freddie Hill. The first had joined City as a junior in 1968, taking Glyn Pardoe's place when the defender had broken his leg.

Willie's first League game for the Blues was on February 7th, 1970 against Nottingham Forest. He was to make 426 appearances for City with whom he stayed until moving to a North American club in 1980.

Colleague Hill moved across the Pennines from Halifax Town in May 1970, staying until his transfer to Peterborough three years later, after representing City on 40 occasions.

The 1971/72 season had new directors at the helm in the shape of Joe Smith and the current chairman Peter Swales.

The Blues finished fourth at the close of the season, one point behind the leaders Derby County. Two players had their two-hundredth League game for the club this season: Mike Doyle on September 1st when Liverpool were beaten 1-0, and Colin Bell on October 30th, the date of a 1-1 draw with Huddersfield.

	Top of Division One 1971/72						
	P	W	D	L	F	A	Pts
Derby	42	24	10	8	69	33	58
Leeds	42	24	9	9	73	31	57
Liverpool	42	24	9	9	64	30	57
Manchester City	42	23	11	8	77	45	57

In the League Cup, City beat Wolves 4-3 at Maine Road. At one stage they were 3-1 down, but they put away three sparkling goals in just six minutes during the second half! Unfortunately the Maine Road side could not maintain this winning streak, and were pushed out of the competition by Bolton in a 3-0 defeat in Round Three.

In the Charity Shield, City defeated Aston Villa 1-0 in front of a 34,860 crowd, and brought the award to Maine Road just four years after last winning the trophy.

Marsh and Davies

The club was eager to sign new players, and so Rodney Marsh and Wyn Davies appeared in the 1971/72 season. The second player was signed for £60,000 from Newcastle, replacing Neil Young, while £200,000 was paid to Queens Park Rangers for Marsh.

Opposite: September 23rd, 1972, and City fought off a rampant Stoke side who eventually won 5-1. Francis Lee scored the only goal for the Blues.

Rodney Marsh

Marsh was born in Hatfield in 1944, and like Summerbee and Lee he added considerable panache to the City squad. An individualist rather than team player, Rodney represented England on eight occasions while with the Maine Road club.

Playing his first game for City against Chelsea on March 18th, 1972, he soon proved himself popular with the crowds, scoring two goals against West Ham United on April 8th in the Blues' 3-1 victory.

In the last game of the 1971/72 season, Marsh and Lee scored one apiece in the 2-0 win over Derby County. This turned out to be an exciting game since Derby were striving to gain top place in Division One. In fact they went on to reach this position with 58 points, while Leeds and Liverpool occupied second and third slots.

During his four years at Maine Road, the resourceful Marsh scored on 46 occasions in a variety of games before departing for Tampa Bay Rowdies in 1976. Rodney later returned to play with Fulham, and is now a highly respected soccer pundit, currently based in the United States.

Wyn Davies

Wyn scored on only two occasions in 34 Division One games in his final season at Newcastle.

This £60,000 signing from the North East club joined a Maine Road squad where Lee, Summerbee and Bell were in their heyday. Davies soon established himself as a strong reliable player who was particularly good in the air.

The Welshman was in fact a quiet person who tried to shun publicity, leaving Maine Road in September 1972 a year or so after joining the Blues. Representing City on 49 occasions, Wyn certainly attracted the media's attention when he departed from Maine Road in order to join rivals United.

Mercer and Allison Leave

In June 1972, Joe Mercer moved to the post of general manager at Coventry. When Joe left Maine Road, Malcolm Allison achieved his ambition of being in control at City.

The next season would be disappointing for the Blues and Allison would be leaving for Crystal Palace. The 1972/73 season started poorly with City winning only two of the first eight League games with Allison in the managerial seat.

The club remained in the relegation zone in Division One until October 21st, 1972 when things began to improve with a 4-3 victory over West Ham. Two more notable wins around this period included a 4-0 defeat of Derby County, plus the convincing 3-0 victory against Manchester United on November 18th, 1972. The Blues displayed a competitive edge in this second game where an opposition own goal and two from Bell gave City the fillip they deserved.

City accomplished little in the 1972/73 League Cup, following a brief interlude in the competition when they enjoyed a run of

Moments to Remember

just two games. The Maine Road side scored four times in the Round Two Rochdale match, but were knocked out 2-0 in Round Three by a Fourth Division Bury side.

The Blues made a promising start to the FA Cup competition, playing Stoke on January 13th 1973. The resulting 3-2 score allowed the Manchester club to meet Liverpool where a 0-0 draw was the result.

In the return match, City's resounding 2-0 victory moved them on to Round Five and Sunderland. The Blues played the North East club on two occasions. The first of these was on January 24th, 1973, where, in a 2-2 draw, Towers was sent off and Sunderland's goalie, Montgomery, scored an own goal!

The Second Division club beat City 3-1 in the replay and went on to lift the Cup, beating Leeds United in the Final.

The end of March witnessed Malcolm Allison's move to Crystal Palace as manager. When Allison vacated the City top spot, Johnny Hart acted as caretaker manager in 1973 when the club came eleventh in Division One, with Liverpool top and Manchester United 18th.

Three Managers in One Season

What an unusual season 1973/74 turned out to be. City experienced not only three managers but also a new chairman, Peter Swales. Allison's successor, Johnny Hart, was already known to older fans, having played for City between 1944 and 1963.

However, after six months in the manager's chair Hart quit because of ill-health.

New boss Ron Saunders moved from Norwich in December 1973, but he too spent only a few months in the hot seat. He left just after City's defeat by Wolves in the League Cup Final.

The faithful retainer, Tony Book, who had been Saunders' assistant, was the next to assume managerial duties. He was just what the club needed – a committed and loyal person who occupied the manager's chair until 1979.

The combination of Swales and Book paid dividends, with City collecting the League Cup in 1976 and becoming runners up in the following year's Division One Championship.

Lee Goes, Law Returns

The early 1970s saw several comings and goings of Maine Road playing staff. Out went Towers in March 1974 when he moved to Sunderland, and in came MacRae, Law, Horswill and Tueart.

Scottish Under-23 'keeper MacRae was bought from Motherwell for £100,000, while the same amount was paid by Saunders to lure Horswill away from Sunderland in March 1974.

For many fans, 1974 was the end of an era, as Francis Lee transferred to Derby County. The talented forward retired from soccer two years later to concentrate on his thriving business ventures.

The Junior Blues Supporters' Club started about this period. Younger fans could now enjoy an organisation which was to be copied by several other English clubs.

July 1973 was a momentous month in Manchester's soccer history. Denis Law rejoined City from rivals Manchester United who had given him a free transfer at the end of the 1972/73 season.

Blues fans could not wait for the distinguished player to turn out on the Maine Road turf. They were not disappointed with this star, who put away nine goals in 22 League games during 1972/73.

Of course the older fans brought to mind Denis's earlier games with City in 1960/1, when the single minded player scored in five out of his first 10 League appearances.

Law's touch of genius persuaded selectors to choose him for the Scottish World Cup squad in 1974 when he played in the opening game against Zaire.

Denis bowed out in spectacular fashion, playing his last game in League soccer against Manchester United on April 27th 1974 in front of an Old Trafford crowd of almost 57,000. Many of us will remember vividly the reaction of United fans as their one-time idol turned out in the sky blue City shirt. The Blues fans cheered on Denis, knowing that a defeat for their rivals would dispatch United into Division Two.

A draw looked like a likely outcome of the game, when suddenly – just minutes from the end – a clever Denis Law back-heel evaded United's Stepney, making the final score 1-0, which forced the Reds into the lower Division. United and their followers were devastated.

Denis Law's illustrious soccer style was a mixture of skilful moves and inspired passing techniques. Although he ceased playing in 1974, Denis still retains an interest in soccer, and today he is a sports commentator and critic.

Dennis Tueart

During Tony Book's reign as manager (1974-79) many players came to the club. Asa Hartford (1974-79), Dave Watson (1975-79), Joe Royle (1974-77) and Dennis Tueart are just some examples.

This last player enjoyed two spells with City – 1974/78 and 1980/83. Moving from Sunderland at the start of his first period with the club, the striker will long be remembered for his role in the 1976 League Cup Final against Newcastle United. Of the 107 goals he put away for City, the most exciting occurred in the Final when his superb overhead kick left 'keeper Mahoney rooted to the spot. There was no doubt about this goal, nor that City deserved to win 2-1.

While at Maine Road, Tueart gained six England caps. He took time out to play for the renowned New York Cosmos club between 1978 and 1980 before returning to Manchester. Dennis eventually left City on a free transfer for Stoke in July 1983.

The League and the F.A. Cup 1973/74

City found themselves in fourteenth place in Division One at the close of the 1973/74 season. However, in the cold January days of 1974, the team was involved in a series of demanding FA Cup and League Cup games.

The Final of the League Cup took place against Wolves on March 3rd 1974 when City were represented by:

MacRae, Pardoe, Donachie, Doyle, Booth, Towers, Summerbee, Bell, Lee, Law and Marsh.

100,000 spectators packed Wembley stadium where the first goal appeared in the 43rd minute giving Wolves that all important 1-0 lead just before the interval. Many City fans who had travelled south for the game felt that their team had had the upper hand in the second half when they produced some invigorating play.

Excitement mounted as Colin Bell expertly converted a Marsh cross into a perfectly timed volley which made it 1-1. Unfortunately for City, just five minutes from the end, Richards rattled in the winner for Wolves to produce a 2-1 victory for the Midlands team.

There was, however, some consolation for City followers. Their club secured the Lancashire Senior Cup following a 3-1 defeat of Morecambe on May 11th 1974. This was the last season of the competition, and the victory meant that City had won the Cup for the sixth time. The other triumphs had been in 1921, 1923, 1928, 1930 and 1953.

Top of Division One

It was soon apparent that manager Tony Book had brought some stability to the club, as November 1974 found the Blues in top slot in Division One.

Sadly this successful run could not be sustained owing to suspensions and injuries. These were hard times for City as the team won only two away games. This was on August 28th, 1974 against Tottenham (2-1), and in the following April when Chelsea went down 1-0.

Mike Summerbee's suspension meant that he had to sit out three matches early in the season. Considerable interest was generated by Rodney Marsh who began the year well as captain, scoring nine goals during 1974/75.

FA Cup and League Cup games, January 1974			
Date	Competition	Opponents	Result
January 5th	FA Cup (Round Three)	Oxford United	5-2
January 16th	League Cup (Round Five, replay)	Coventry City	4-2
January 23rd	League Cup (Semi-final) 1st Leg	Plymouth Argyle	1-1
January 26th	FA Cup (Round Four)	Notts County	1-4
January 30th	League Cup (Semi-final) 2nd Leg	Plymouth Argyle	2-0 (Agg.3-1)

Scunthorpe United were propping up the Fourth Division when they visited Maine Road, only to be humiliated in a 6-0 defeat in Round Two of the League Cup. The next match in the competition paired the Blues with Manchester United in Round Three. The venue was at the Reds' ground on October 9th 1974.

The Reds came out on top as a Daly penalty saw them through to Round Four with a score of 1-0.

United made it to the Semi-final of the League Cup where they lost 2-3 on aggregate.

City were pleasantly surprised by an FA ruling which decreed that Round Three of the FA Cup against Newcastle should take place at Maine Road. Although the Blues had been drawn away, the North East club's crowd problems meant that the venue had to be switched. But in spite of playing in front of a mainly home audience, City lost 2-0 in the January 4th clash.

New Blood in the mid-1970s

In the mid 1970s Tony Book realised that new blood was required in the squad. As a result of his efforts, Asa Hartford, Joe Royle and Geoff Hammond donned sky blue shirts in 1974.

Hammond moved from Ipswich for a £40,000 fee in October, while West Bromwich received £250,000 for Asa Hartford a couple of months earlier. Joe Royle transferred from Everton in December 1974. When Scottish international Hartford was on the verge of joining Leeds in 1972, a routine medical revealed that he had a slight heart ailment. This did not deter City, who gladly paid a quarter of a million pounds to West Bromwich Albion for a man whose matchless energy and superb skills indicated that he was in good shape. Asa's performance was exemplary.

Making his League debut for City in August 1974 against West Ham, Hartford totted up 36 goals for City in Cup and League games.

Sold to Nottingham Forest in June 1979, Asa later moved to Everton. It was from the Merseyside club that City bought him once more in 1981, this time for £350,000. The tough, selfless player crossed the Atlantic three years later to join the ranks of the soccer team, Fort Lauderdale Sun, but is now back home, continuing his involvement with the game as a coach.

Tony Book paid in the region of £180,000 for yet another Everton signing, Joe Royle, who had spent a decade with the Merseyside Club before trying his fortunes at Maine Road. "Big Joe" displayed impressive aerial ability and made important contributions to City's success in the 1970s.

He eventually transferred to Bristol City in December 1977, and then went to Norwich. In the early 1990s, Liverpool born Joe is manager of Oldham Athletic.

Hailing from Winsford and playing for City between 1958 and 1976, Alan Oakes made an important contribution to the Blues' golden era of the 1970s. His loyal, unstinting

Opposite: In 1976/77, City displayed a competitive edge which more than satisfied their fans. They did not lose a League game between October 2nd and February 16th.

service was rewarded by a Testimonial match against United in 1972.

To commemorate his 500th appearance for the club, Alan was presented with a silver memento before the Stoke game on November 9th, 1974. Two years later he became player-manager at Chester.

1976 League Cup Final

The 1975/76 season was memorable for the victory over Newcastle United in the League Cup, this being City's third appearance in the Final in seven years.

The Maine Road side had beaten Norwich, Nottingham Forest, Manchester United, Mansfield Town and Middlesbrough before reaching Wembley. Needless to say the 4-0 victory over Old Trafford rivals caused quite a stir amongst the City ranks.

As a point of interest, when the two clubs met in League games, a 2-2 draw was the outcome on September 27th, while in the last game of the season on May 4th, City lost 2-0.

The Tynesiders were affected by a flu epidemic, but they could still field Malcolm Macdonald to worry City's defence.

Barnes opened the scoring for the Maine Road side with Gowling equalising for the 'Magpies'. There then followed a spectacular overhead kick by Dennis Tueart that settled the issue for the Blues, who enjoyed a 2-1 victory, thereby avenging the FA Cup defeat at the hands of Newcastle in 1955.

The League 1975/76

The Blues were eighth again in this season, the same as the previous year.

The first team squad was now quite different from a couple of seasons earlier. Mike Summerbee transferred to Burnley in June 1975, later moving to Blackpool and then Stockport County. And it was in this month that the powerful centre half, Dave Watson, signed on at Maine Road from Sunderland, in a £200,000 deal.

1976/77 Season

In 1976/77, City looked to build on their League Cup success against Newcastle United, and gave their fans some heart-stopping moments. Two defeats in the first 25 games was impressive proof of the talent that Tony Book had assembled at Maine Road. Hopes were high that the League title would be within their grasp.

Top of Division One 1976/77

	P	W	D	L	F	A	Pts
Liverpool	42	23	11	8	62	33	57
Manchester City	42	21	14	7	60	34	56
Ipswich Town	42	22	8	12	66	39	56

Moments to Remember

		Arsenal	Aston Villa	Birmingham City	Bristol City	Coventry City	Derby County	Everton	Ipswich Town	Leeds United	Leicester City	Liverpool	Manchester City	Manchester United	Middlesborough	Newcastle United	Norwich City	Queen's Park Rangers	Stoke City	Sunderland	Tottenham Hotspur	West Bromwich Albion	West Ham United		
Arsenal	H		3-0	4-0	0-1	2-0	0-0	3-1	1-4	1-1	3-0	1-1	0-0	3-1	1-1	5-3	1-0	3-2	2-0	0-0	1-0	1-2	2-3	H	Arsenal
	A		1-5	3-3	0-2	2-1	0-0	1-2	1-3	1-2	1-4	0-2	0-1	2-3	0-3	2-0	3-1	1-2	1-1	2-2	2-2	2-0	2-0	A	
Aston Villa	H	5-1		1-2	3-1	2-2	4-0	2-0	5-2	2-1	2-0	5-1	1-1	3-2	1-0	2-1	1-0	1-1	1-0	4-1	2-1	4-0	4-0	H	Aston Villa
	A	0-3		1-2	0-0	3-2	1-2	2-0	0-1	3-1	1-1	0-3	0-2	0-2	2-3	2-3	1-1	1-2	0-1	1-0	1-3	1-1	1-0	A	
Birmingham City	H	3-3	2-1		3-0	3-1	5-1	1-1	2-4	0-0	1-1	2-1	0-0	2-3	3-1	1-2	3-2	2-1	2-0	2-0	1-2	0-1	0-0	H	Birmingham City
	A	0-4	2-1		1-0	1-2	0-0	2-2	0-1	0-1	6-2	1-4	1-2	2-2	2-2	2-3	0-1	2-2	0-1	0-1	0-1	1-2	2-2	A	
Bristol City	H	2-0	0-0	0-1		0-0	2-2	1-2	1-2	1-0	0-1	2-1	1-0	1-1	1-2	1-1	3-1	1-0	1-1	4-1	1-0	1-2	1-1	H	Bristol City
	A	1-0	1-3	0-3		2-2	0-2	0-2	0-1	0-2	0-0	1-2	1-2	0-0	0-0	1-2	1-0	2-2	0-1	1-0	1-1	0-2	0-2	A	
Coventry City	H	1-2	2-3	2-1	2-2		2-0	4-2	1-1	4-2	1-1	0-0	0-1	0-2	1-1	1-1	2-0	2-0	5-2	1-2	1-1	1-1	1-1	H	Coventry City
	A	0-2	2-2	1-3	0-0		1-1	1-1	1-2	2-1	1-3	1-3	0-2	0-2	0-1	0-1	0-3	1-1	0-2	1-0	1-0	1-1	0-2	A	
Derby County	H	0-0	2-1	0-0	2-0	1-1		2-3	0-0	0-1	1-0	2-3	4-0	0-0	0-0	4-2	2-2	2-0	2-0	1-0	8-2	2-2	1-1	H	Derby County
	A	0-0	0-4	1-5	2-2	0-2		0-2	0-0	0-1	0-2	1-1	1-3	2-3	1-3	0-2	2-2	0-0	1-1	0-1	1-1	0-0	0-1	2-2	A	
Everton	H	2-1	0-2	2-2	2-0	1-1	2-0		1-1	0-2	1-2	0-0	2-2	1-2	2-2	2-0	3-1	1-3	3-0	2-0	4-0	1-1	3-2	H	Everton
	A	1-3	0-2	1-1	2-1	2-4	3-2		0-2	0-0	1-1	1-3	1-1	0-4	2-1	1-4	2-2	1-1	1-2	4-0	1-0	3-3	0-3	2-2	A	
Ipswich Town	H	3-1	1-0	1-0	1-0	2-1	0-0	2-0		1-1	0-0	1-0	2-1	0-1	2-0	5-0	2-2	0-1	3-1	3-1	7-0	4-1		H	Ipswich Town
	A	4-1	2-5	4-2	2-1	1-1	0-0	1-1		1-2	0-1	1-2	1-2	1-0	2-0	1-1	1-0	0-1	1-2	0-1	0-1	0-4	2-0	A	
Leeds United	H	2-1	1-3	1-0	2-0	1-2	2-0	0-0	2-1		2-2	1-1	0-2	0-2	2-1	2-2	3-0	0-1	1-1	1-1	2-1	2-2	1-1	H	Leeds United
	A	1-1	1-2	0-0	0-1	2-4	1-0	2-0	1-1		1-0	1-3	1-2	0-1	0-1	0-3	2-1	0-1	1-2	1-0	0-1	2-1	3-1	A	
Leicester City	H	4-1	1-1	2-6	0-0	3-1	1-1	1-1	1-0	0-1		0-1	2-2	1-1	3-3	1-0	1-1	2-2	1-0	2-0	2-1	0-5	2-0	H	Leicester City
	A	0-3	0-2	1-1	1-0	1-1	0-1	2-1	0-0	2-2		1-5	0-5	1-1	1-0	0-0	2-3	1-3	0-0	0-2	2-2	0-0	0-1	A	
Liverpool	H	2-0	3-0	4-1	2-1	3-1	3-1	3-1	2-1	3-1	5-1		2-1	1-0	0-0	1-0	3-1	4-0	2-0	1-1	0-0		H	Liverpool
	A	1-1	1-5	1-2	1-2	0-0	3-2	0-0	0-1	1-1	1-0		1-1	0-0	1-0	1-2	1-1	0-0	1-0	0-1	1-0	0-2	A	
Manchester City	H	1-0	2-0	2-1	2-1	2-0	3-2	1-1	2-1	5-0	1-1	1-3		1-0	0-0	0-0	1-0	5-0	1-0	4-2	H	Manchester City
	A	0-0	1-1	0-0	0-1	1-0	0-4	2-2	0-1	2-0	2-2	1-2		1-3	0-0	2-2	2-0	0-0	2-0	2-2	2-0	0-1	A	
Manchester United	H	3-2	2-0	2-2	2-1	2-0	3-1	4-0	0-1	1-0	1-1	0-0	3-1		2-0	3-1	2-2	1-0	3-0	3-3	2-3	2-2	0-2	H	Manchester United
	A	1-3	2-3	3-2	1-1	2-0	0-0	2-1	1-2	2-0	1-1	0-1	3-1		0-3	2-0	0-4	3-1	2-1	3-1	0-4	2-4	A	
Middlesborough	H	3-0	3-2	2-2	0-0	1-0	2-2	2-2	0-2	1-0	0-1	0-1	0-0	3-0		1-0	1-0	0-2	0-0	2-1	2-0	1-0	1-1	H	Middlesborough
	A	1-1	0-1	1-3	2-1	1-1	0-0	2-2	1-0	1-2	3-3	0-0	0-1	0-2		0-1	0-3	1-3	0-4	0-0	1-2	1-0	A	
Newcastle United	H	0-2	3-2	2-2	0-0	1-0	2-2	4-1	1-1	3-0	0-0	1-0	2-2	2-2	1-0		5-1	2-0	1-0	2-0	2-0	3-0	H	Newcastle United
	A	3-5	1-2	2-1	1-1	1-1	2-4	0-2	0-2	2-2	0-1	0-1	0-0	1-3	0-1		2-3	2-1	0-0	2-2	0-0	1-1	2-1	A	
Norwich City	H	1-3	1-1	1-0	2-1	3-0	0-0	2-1	0-1	1-2	3-2	2-1	0-2	2-1	1-0	3-2		2-0	1-1	2-2	1-3	1-0	1-0	H	Norwich City
	A	0-1	0-1	2-3	103	0-2	2-2	1-3	0-5	2-3	1-1	0-1	0-2	2-2	0-1	1-5		3-2	0-0	1-1	0-2	0-1	0-1	A	
Queen's Park Rangers	H	2-1	2-1	2-2	0-1	1-1	1-1	0-4	1-0	0-0	3-2	1-1	0-0	4-0	3-0	1-2	2-3		2-0	2-0	2-1	1-0	1-1	H	Queen's Park Rangers
	A	2-3	1-1	1-2	0-1	0-2	0-2	3-1	2-2	1-0	2-2	1-3	0-0	0-1	2-0	0-2	0-2		0-1	0-1	0-3	1-1	0-1	A	
Stoke City	H	1-1	1-0	1-0	2-2	2-0	1-0	0-1	2-1	2-1	0-1	0-0	2-2	3-3	3-1	0-0	0-0	1-0		0-0	0-0	2-1	H	Stoke City
	A	0-2	0-1	0-2	1-1	2-5	0-2	0-3	1-0	1-1	0-1	0-4	0-0	0-3	0-0	0-1	1-1	0-2		0-0	0-2	1-3	0-1	A	
Sunderland	H	2-2	0-1	1-0	1-0	0-1	1-1	0-1	1-0	0-1	0-0	0-1	0-2	1-2	4-0	2-2	0-1	1-0	0-0		2-1	6-1	6-0	H	Sunderland
	A	0-0	1-4	0-2	1-4	2-1	0-0	0-2	1-3	1-1	0-2	0-1	3-3	1-2	0-2	2-2	0-2	0-0		1-1	3-2	1-1	A	
Tottenham Hotspur	H	2-2	3-1	1-0	0-1	0-1	0-0	3-3	1-0	1-0	2-0	1-0	2-2	1-3	0-0	2-0	1-1	3-0	2-0	1-1		0-2	2-1	H	Tottenham Hotspur
	A	0-1	1-2	2-1	1-0	1-1	2-8	0-4	1-3	1-2	0-2	0-5	3-2	0-2	3-1	1-2	1-0	1-2		2-4	3-5	A	
West Bromwich Albion	H	0-2	1-1	2-1	1-1	1-1	1-0	3-0	4-0	1-2	2-2	0-1	0-2	4-0	2-1	1-1	2-0	1-1	3-1	2-3	4-2		3-0	H	West Bromwich Albion
	A	2-1	0-4	1-0	2-1	1-1	2-2	1-1	0-7	2-2	5-0	1-1	0-1	2-2	0-1	0-2	0-1	2-0	1-6	2-0		0-0	A	
West Ham United	H	0-2	0-1	2-2	2-0	2-0	2-2	0-2	1-3	0-0	2-0	1-0	4-2	0-1	1-2	1-0	1-0	0-1	1-1	5-3	0-0		H	West Ham United
	A	3-2	0-4	0-0	1-1	1-1	1-1	2-3	1-4	0-2	0-0	2-4	2-0	1-0	0-3	0-1	1-1	1-2	0-6	1-2	0-3		A	

Opposite: Stoke-v-Manchester City League game on February 5th 1977, when goals by Royle and Tueart gave the Blues a 2-1 victory as City exploited Stoke's weaknesses.

Below: The U.E.F.A. Cup 1978/79 produced a run of three matches, until City were knocked out in the Quarter-finals.

However, a 1-2 defeat against Liverpool at Anfield on Easter Saturday was to be crucial as the Merseyside club eventually pipped City for the Championship by just one point.

League and FA Cup Problems 1977-80

There was another successful League run in 1977/78, City coming fourth in Division One when the average gate was 42,000. Unfortunately this did not continue into the next season which brought fifteenth place, while by 1979/80 the club had dropped to seventeenth slot. This was their lowest position since 1966/67, when they were fifteenth.

During 1977/78, the Blues reached Round Four of the F.A. Cup only to be knocked out 2-1 by Nottingham Forest. In the following season's F.A. Cup saga there was that shock defeat by Third Division Shrewsbury Town on January 27th, 1979.

City had a few problems around this period. Halifax beat them in an F.A. Cup match on January 5th 1980, and this quashed any hopes they might have entertained of winning the cup. Following the defeat of Everton on December 22nd, 1979 City did not win again until they beat Wolves 2-1 on April 12th.

European Soccer in the late 1970s

The Maine Road club had only a brief encounter with continental soccer in the late 1970s, when the crack side Juventus defeated the Blues 2-1 on aggregate. This was in the initial round of the 1976/77 U.E.F.A. competition — the first time they had played in this since the 1972/73 season.

Fortunately, the Manchester team was placed second in Division One in 1977, just behind Liverpool. This allowed City to have another crack at European soccer the following year. However, 1977/78 brought only a minor flirtation as City were forced out of the U.E.F.A. Cup by a hitherto unknown Polish side – Widzew Lodz. The Blues lost on the away goals rule, having drawn 2-2 in the First Leg, and 0-0 in the second meeting.

Sixteenth-Final		Eighth-Final		Quarter-Final		Semi-Final		Final	
Bor. M'N'G'Bach	0:2	Bor. M'N'G'Bach	1:4	Bor. M'N'G'Bach	1:3				
Benfica	0:0					Bor. M'N'G'Bach	2:4		
Slask Wroclaw	2:2	Slask Wroclaw	1:2						
IBV Westmann	0:1								
Manchester City	4:0	Manchester City	2:3	Manchester City	1:1				
Standard Liege	0:2							Bor. M'N'G'Bach	1:1
AC Milan	1:3	A. C. Milan	2:0						
Levski Spartak	1:0								
MSV Duisburg	0:3	MSV Duisburg	0:4	MSV Duisburg†	3:1				
Carl Zeiss Jena	0:0					MSV Duisburg	2:1		
Strasbourg	2:0	Strasbourg	0:0						
Hibernian	0:1								
Honved	4:0	Honved	4:0	Honved	2:2				
Polit Timisoara	0:2								
Ajax	1:4	Ajax	1:2					First leg in Belgrade	
Lausanne	0:0							Second leg in Duesseldorf	
Hertha Berlin	2:0	Hertha Berlin	1:4	Hertha Berlin	1:2				
Dynamo Tbilisi	0:1					Hertha Berlin	0:2		
Esbjerg	2:4	Esbjerg	2:0						
Kuopio Palloseura	0:1								
Dukla Prague†	1:1	Dukla Prague	1:4	Dukla Prague	1:1				
Everton	2:0								
VFB Stuttgart	1:2	VFB Stuttgart	4:0					Red Star Bel.	1:0
Moscow Torpedo	2:0								
West Brom. Alb.	2:1	West Brom. Alb.	1:2	West Brom. Alb.	0:1				
Sporting Braga	0:0								
Valencia	1:5	Valencia	1:0			Red Star Bel.†	1:1		
Arges Pitesti	2:2								
Arsenal†	1:1	Arsenal	0:1	Red Star Bel.	1:1				
Hajduk Split	2:0								
Sporting Gijon	0:1	Red Star Bel.	1:1						
Red Star Belgrade	1:1								

† Won on away goals counting double

Manchester City

Considerable excitement was generated by the 1978/79 U.E.F.A. clashes with Twente Enschede, Standard Liège and AC Milan. A 5-2 aggregate score against this last Italian club took City on to Round Four.

But after drawing 1-1 at home to Borussia Mönchengladbach, the Blues went down 3-1 in the Second Leg in West Germany.

Arrivals & Departures 1977-79

City embarked on a large spending spree for new players to replace those who were leaving. Fans were concerned about an exodus of good players, and they hoped that Malcolm Allison and Tony Book would replace them with comparable talent.

So who actually came to Maine Road in the late 1970s? Remember Deyna, Daley, Silkman, Tueart (again), and Dragoslav Stepanovic who moved from the West German club Wormatia in August 1979?

The fans watched with interest the arrival of 30 year old Polish international Kazimiera Deyna, who transferred from Legia Warsaw.

A fee of £120,000 was paid for him in November 1978. Deyna stayed with his new club until January 1981, when he moved to the San Diego Football Club.

After all these changes, a typical squad was the one fielded against Sunderland on October 3rd, 1979. The following players turned out for City in a Round Three replay of the League Cup, which City lost 1-0:

Corrigan, Ranson, Donachie, Stepanovic, Caton, Futcher, MacKenzie, Daley, Robinson, Power, Deyna

Examples of players who left in the late 1970s

	Date of Leaving	New Club
Royle	December 1977	Bristol City
Conway	January 1978	Portland Timbers
Tueart	February 1978	New York Cosmos
Doyle	June 1978	Stoke City
Kidd	March 1979	Everton
Watson	June 1979	Werder Bremen
Bell	August 1979	Retired
Channon	September 1979	Southampton
Clements	September 1979	Oldham

Examples of new players in the late 1970s

	Previous Club and Fee	Date of signing for City
Kazimiera Deyna	Legia Warsaw (£120,000)	November 1978
Mick Robinson	Preston North End (£750,000)	June 1979
Steve Daley	Wolves (£1.4 million)	September 1979
Dennis Tueart	New York Cosmos (£150,000)	January 1980
Kevin Reeves	Norwich City (£1.2 million)	March 1980

7

1980 – 1990

Bond to the Rescue?

The first dozen games of 1980/81 did not bring a single win for City. Allison and Book relinquished their posts at Maine Road, with Malcolm taking on a number of soccer jobs in the UK and abroad, while Tony Book went to join Cardiff City before returning to Maine Road as coach in the summer of 1981.

With Book and Allison out, John Bond moved into the manager's post at Maine Road, arriving from Norwich in October 1980. His background was impressive. He had played for West Ham and Torquay, later managing Bournemouth and Norwich, both of whom were promoted when he was boss.

Maine Road now had another double act at the top as Bond's assistant, John Benson, provided support for the new manager.

Gerry Gow was bought from Bristol City, while Bobby McDonald and Tommy Hutchison moved from Coventry City.

Joining City in 1980, Tueart and Reeves stayed until July 1983, while Gow represented City until 1982, making almost 40 appearances and scoring seven goals before moving to Rotherham United. McDonald's City career lasted until September 1983 when Oxford United beckoned him, while Hutchison had sought his fortune with a Hong Kong club a year earlier.

City fans may also remember Phil Boyer whose reign lasted from November 1980 until his retirement in September 1983. Another departure in the early 1980s was goalkeeper MacRae who made 71 appearances before trying his luck with Portland Timbers in 1981, having served City since 1973.

The Blues did not win a League game until their thirteenth fixture of 1980/81 when Spurs were defeated 3-1 on October 22nd. But John Bond's presence stirred things up, since between November 15th and January 17th, the Blues lost only one of 10 League matches. This was against Tottenham when the London side won 2-1. City were finding their feet again, notching up good wins against Leeds (1-0), Everton (2-0) and Wolves (4-0) in three consecutive League games in December 1980.

The local derby had its usual attraction, a 2-2 draw resulting from the September clash of the old rivals. A MacKenzie goal clinched victory for City who won 1-0 in front of 50,000 spectators in February 1981.

John Bond managed to keep his club out of the relegation zone with City positioned twelfth in 1981. This was the highest they had been for a few seasons – 15th in 1979, and 17th in 1980.

The FA Cup Competition 1981

The Way to Wembley

Bond mania was much in evidence as his club reached the Semi-final of the League Cup and then became 1981 FA Cup finalists for the eighth time in City's history.

The run-up to the FA Cup attracted considerable media interest since the Blues tackled Allison's club Crystal Palace, plus John Bond's former Norwich City side.

In the first of these encounters, almost 40,000 fans packed into Maine Road as Malcolm Allison's squad was beaten 4-0. Reeves pushed in two goals, Power one, while Boyer provided the fourth.

Ironically, the next round saw John Bond's former club facing Manchester City. This confrontation stayed in fans' minds for a number of reasons. There was the tackle on Phil Boyer which damaged his knee ligament, but also the outstanding achievement of the Blues' resounding 6-0 victory.

Peterborough were the next to succumb to City in Round Five, while the first clash with Everton on March 7th resulted in a 2-2 draw. Gow scored for City in the first half while Eastoe provided one for the Merseysiders. In the second half, Ross put Everton 2-1 up from a penalty kick, but the Blues summoned up a further act of defiance when Power found the back of the Everton net in the last five minutes of a gruelling game.

In the Maine Road replay, City ensured they had a place in the Semi-final thanks to efforts by McDonald, who scored twice, while Power supplied a third in the 3-1 victory.

In the Semi-final, Ipswich were hoping for The Treble, but had to give up all hopes of this when an extra time goal by Power took the Blues to the Final following a 1-0 Semi-final victory.

The FA Cup Final -v- Spurs

On May 9th, 1981, these players represented City against Spurs in the FA Cup Final:

Corrigan, Ranson, McDonald, Reid, Power, Caton, Bennett, Gow, MacKenzie, Hutchison, Reeves

At the end of the first half hour in this centenary final, Hutchison latched on to a Ranson cross and headed the ball home. The fans held their breath – could City hold on to this slender 1-0 lead?

Sadly this was not to be the case. Sympathy must go out to City's Hutchison when a deflected ball hit him, beat Corrigan, and

Route to the 1981 FA Cup Final

Round	Date	Opponents	Result
3	January 3rd	Crystal Palace	4-0
4	January 24th	Norwich City	6-0
5	Feb 14th	Peterborough United	1-0
6	March 7th	Everton	2-2
6 (Replay)	March 11th	Everton	3-1
Semi-final	April 11th	Ipswich Town	1-0
Final	May 9th	Tottenham	1-1
Final (Replay)	May 14th	Tottenham	2-3

produced an own goal. The 1-1 result necessitated a replay five days later.

So, out came the two sides on May 14th for a game watched by almost 93,000 spectators at Wembley. They were rewarded with early goals as Villa scored for Spurs in the first ten minutes. A couple of minutes later, however, City equalised with a devastating shot by MacKenzie who converted a Hutchison header.

The score remained 1-1 until five minutes after half time. Following a foul on Bennett, Reeves smacked in a penalty to give the Blues the lead. A seventieth minute leveller by Crooks made it 2-2, and then Villa slipped a clever goal past Corrigan, ensuring the F.A. Cup would find a home in Tottenham's trophy case.

Although failing to secure the Cup, City fans enjoyed a scintillating Final which had kept them on the edge of their seats until the ninetieth minute whistle.

The League Cup and the League

In 1980/81 City appeared in a number of exciting matches in the run-up to the Semi-final of the League Cup. They had eliminated Stoke, Luton Town, Notts County and West Bromwich Albion before the Semi-final encounter with Liverpool.

The first leg was held at Maine Road on January 14th, 1981. It resulted in a 1-0 victory for Liverpool, much to the annoyance of City followers who disagreed with the referee when a Reeves goal was disallowed.

In the Anfield leg of the semi-final, Dalglish made it 2-0 on aggregate. However, the talented MacKenzie managed to twist a free kick around the defensive line, and Reeves pushed the ball into the net.

The Blues' fans urged on their team as a Bennett shot crashed against the bar, but City could not prevent Liverpool from winning 2-1 on aggregate. The City faithful made their way back to Manchester, trying to put the game behind them, and hoping for better things in the F.A. Cup tie with Peterborough four days later. As we have seen, this February 14th meeting culminated in a 1-0 victory for City.

At the start of the 1981/82 season City were chasing Division One leaders, Swansea, the final League position seeing the Blues occupying 10th place. In the following year, City had nose-dived to 20th slot, just above Swansea. This meant Division Two soccer for the Maine Road club in 1983/84.

Bottom of Division One 1982/83							
	P	W	D	L	F	A	Pts
Manchester City	42	13	8	21	47	70	47
Swansea	42	10	11	21	51	69	41
Brighton	42	9	13	20	38	67	40

In the F.A. Cup, City beat Cardiff City 3-1 in January 1982, but went down to Coventry City by the same score in Round Four. Not much success either in the League Cup, when the Blues were pushed out of the competition in Round Four by Barnsley's 1-0 victory.

More Comings and Goings

The early 1980s proved to be a difficult period in City's history, as several players plus manager John Bond left Maine Road between 1981 and 1983.

1982/83 in particular was an upsetting time as City lost 4-0 to Brighton in an FA Cup tie. This was followed almost immediately by the resignation of manager John Bond. The 1981/83 period also brought several new signings to Maine Road.

Perhaps one of the most attractive players from this list was the talented Trevor Francis, signed for £1.2 million from Nottingham Forest.

Naturally enough, fans hoped the new faces on the pitch would help to revive City, and Trevor did not disappoint them, becoming a firm favourite with the Maine Road faithful.

He scored two goals in the first match he played. This was against Stoke on September 5th, 1981 when Boyer's contribution made it 3-1 for the Blues

Trevor Francis was capped 52 times by England and has subsequently managed Queens Park Rangers and Sheffield Wednesday. He was Britain's first £1 million player in 1979 when he moved to Nottingham Forest.

(The City -v- Sheffield Wednesday League game on September 14th, 1991 featured a *tête-à-tête* between Peter Reid and Trevor Francis as the teams were warming up. Quite an interesting sight as the only two player-managers in Division One discussed old times – Trevor signed Peter for Q.P.R. when the former was manager.)

Another intriguing acquisition around this time was the manager's son, Kevin Bond who came from Seattle Sounders in September 1981. Kevin remained on City's books until his transfer to Southampton in September 1984.

The ever-popular Joe Corrigan had come to Maine Road from Sale F.C. in 1966, making his League debut in March 1969. Joe proved himself in the mid-1970s and went on to win nine England caps, one England under-23 cap and three England under-21 awards. He left Maine Road in Spring 1983, when he moved to Seattle Sounders.

Examples of new players 1981/83

	Date Signed	Date Left	New Club
O'Neill	July 1981	January 1982	Norwich City
Francis	September 1981	July 1982	Sampdoria
K. Bond	September 1981	September 1984	Southampton
Hareide	October 1981	July 1983	Norwich City
Ryan	January 1982	July 1983	Stockport County
Cross	July 1982	April 1983	Vancouver Whitecaps

Superb striker Tueart had two periods with the Blues (1974/78, 1980/83) during which he gained half a dozen England caps. In July 1983, Dennis moved to Stoke City on a free transfer. It was in this year that Caton departed for Arsenal, while Reeves travelled to Burnley in July 1983.

Following John Bond's departure in February 1983, John Benson was left holding the baby. The Blues let him go in June of the same year and replaced him with Billy McNeill. New boss McNeill stayed at the helm for three years following his arrival in 1983. He had been manager of Clyde, Aberdeen and Celtic, and boasted 29 full Scottish caps.

City were twentieth in Division One at the end of 1983 and went into the Second Division, remaining there until their promotion in 1985.

The mid-1980s

Like all new managers, McNeill looked around for fresh players, signing Scottish under-21 international Neil McNab, Jim Tolmie (Lokeren) and Derek Parlane (Leeds). Tony Cunningham transferred from Sheffield Wednesday (July 1984) while David Phillips came from Plymouth in the same month.

Other new arrivals included David Johnson on a free transfer from Everton, and Gordon Smith for whom Brighton received £35,000.

The partnership of Billy McNeill and assistant Jimmy Frizzell was viewed with optimism by the club and fans, but there was little cause for excitement in the early half of the 1984/85 season.

However, as the end of the year approached, promotion looked a definite possibility as City defeated Wolves 4-0 on December 29th. The Blues went on to lose only one of the next 10 League games.

Promotion would be guaranteed if City could win the last League game, which was against Charlton Athletic on May 11th, 1985. Over 47,000 people packed into Maine Road as City moved into Division One in style, thrashing Charlton 5-1 with contributions from May, Phillips (2), Simpson and Melrose. The Blues' relentless pursuit of Division One status had paid dividends as they finished third out of 22 Second Division sides.

City knocked Blackpool and West Ham out of the League Cup in the autumn of 1984, but Chelsea quashed their chances of progressing past Round Four. The Manchester club was beaten 4-1 by the Londoners on November 21st.

Although the start of a new year saw Leeds and City draw 1-1 in a January 1st League game, the Blues achieved little in terms of F.A. Cup success. Four days after the Leeds match, Coventry defeated City 2-1 in Round Three, even though many considered the Blues to be the better side on the day.

Opposite: A piece of drama from the famous 10-1 defeat of Huddersfield Town. The inadequacy of the Yorkshire defence was ruthlessly exposed by a City team, who were in a class of their own.

Division One Soccer 1985/86

City's third position in the 1984/85 Division Two table gained them promotion. Initially, the team seemed to find it hard to acclimatise to Division One winning only two of the first 16 games. These victories were in August 1985 against West Bromwich Albion (3-2) and Spurs (2-1).

They had to wait until November 16th 1985 for the next League win when Nottingham Forest were sent packing 2-0, thanks to contributions by Wilson and Simpson.

Following a successful run in the League Cup, City only went out of the competition after a 2-1 defeat by Arsenal. In the Full Members' Cup, the Blues did reach Wembley. City had shown their professionalism and skills in this competition. There was that incredible 6-1 defeat of Leeds United, followed by a 2-1 win over Sheffield United.

A 0-0 draw with Sunderland was settled by penalties and then the Blues took on Hull City. In the first encounter, they lost 1-2 but in the second leg, the Maine Road side won 2-0. This gave City an aggregate score of 3-2.

A superb Final against Chelsea resulted in a narrow 5-4 victory for the Londoners.

The F.A. Cup was a different matter, as City fans saw their side struggling with Watford, losing 3-1 in a second replay.

Frizzell in Charge

Manager McNeill departed for Aston Villa in September 1986 leaving assistant Jimmy Frizzell as the Maine Road boss. Could he keep the Blues out of Division Two? After all, Frizzell had guided Oldham from the Fourth Division to the Second.

He signed Imre Varadi from West Bromwich Albion in October 1986, while Paul Stewart moved from Blackpool in March 1987. They certainly proved their worth, scoring 48 League and Cup goals in the 1987/88 season. Unfortunately, in 1986/87 City had slipped to twenty-first slot in Division One, and they were destined for Second Division soccer once again.

Perhaps the highlights of this period were the United-City derby games. The Blues drew 1-1 on October 26th but lost 2-0 in March 1987. City's only F.A. Cup tie in 1986/87 took place against rivals United at Old Trafford where a crowd of 54,000 saw the home side win 1-0.

City also had a disappointment in the League Cup, losing 3-1 to Arsenal in Round Three on October 28th.

City 10, Huddersfield 1

Relegation brought the by now familiar reshuffle of the Maine Road hierarchy. Jimmy Frizzell moved to the general manager's post, while Mel Machin became the new team manager. He had been a player at Port Vale, Gillingham and Norwich, later acting as coach for this last club.

In 1987/88 the highest position attained by City in Division Two was fifth, the close of the season seeing the Blues in ninth place.

Moments to Remember

Manchester City

Opposite: Liverpool goalkeeper, Bruce Grobbelaar pulls off a save in the March 1988 F.A. Cup match against City. The Merseyside team won 4-0 in front of a Maine Road crowd of 44,000, who had turned out to enjoy this Sixth Round tie.

The most remarkable fixture of the season was the one with Huddersfield when the Manchester club won 10-1. This ferocious attack on the Yorkshire side occurred on November 7th, 1987 during a Division Two League game.

No doubt Huddersfield 'keeper Brian Cox vividly recalls the 10 goals, but he proved his worth on January 12th when he kept the Blues off the score sheet in the 0-0 draw in a Round Three replay of the FA Cup, and again on April 2nd, when City had a narrow 1-0 defeat by the Yorkshire side.

The FA Cup and the Littlewoods Cup

Even though in Division Two, City could still deliver the goods when it came to Cup matches, reaching the Quarter finals in both the FA Cup and Littlewoods Cup.

The financial gain from these competitions was considerable, with just under half a million pounds going into City's accounts.

The FA Cup

The City fans were treated to seven FA Cup matches in the 1987/88 attempt to reach Wembley.

Paul Stewart must have experienced mixed emotions in the two games with his old club, Blackpool. However, this did not prevent him from scoring in the February 3rd replay.

The Littlewoods Cup

As a Second Division club, City conquered a couple of Division One sides in Rounds Three and Four of the Littlewoods Cup, but were defeated by Everton on January 20th.

The FA Cup 1987/88

Round	Date	Opponents	Result	Scorers
Three	January 9th	Huddersfield Town	2-2	Brightwell; Gildman
Three (Replay)	January 12th	Huddersfield Town	0-0	
Three (Second Replay)	January 25th	Huddersfield Town	3-0	White; Varadi; Hinchcliffe
Four	January 30th	Blackpool	1-1	Lake
Four (Replay)	February 3rd	Blackpool	2-1	Stewart; Simpson
Five	February 20th	Plymouth Argyle	3-1	Scott; Simpson; Moulden
Six	March 13th	Liverpool	0-4	

The 1987/88 Littlewoods Cup

Round	Date	Opponents	Result	Scorers
Two (First leg)	22nd Sept	Wolves	1-2	Adcock
Two (2nd Leg)	6th Oct	Wolves	2-0	Hinchcliffe; Gidman
Three	27th Oct	Nottm Forest	3-0	Varadi (2); Stewart
Four	17th Nov	Watford	3-1	White (2); Stewart
Five	20th Jan	Everton	0-2	

Moments to Remember

New Signing – Andy Dibble

Andy transferred to City on payment of a £240,000 fee to Luton Town. His first game for the Blues was against Hull City on August 27th, 1988.

He had considerable experience as a goalkeeper, playing for Cardiff City and Luton Town plus loan spells at Sunderland and Huddersfield Town, before his move to Maine Road.

It was during his time at Kenilworth Road that Andy made the headlines, executing a brilliant penalty save when his team battled it out with Arsenal in the Littlewoods Cup at Wembley.

When 'keeper Tony Coton arrived at Maine Road in August 1990, Dibble went on loan to Aberdeen and Middlesbrough.

February 1991 saw Andy starting his loan period with Middlesbrough who had Stephen Pears out of action for six weeks after breaking a finger. Andy maintained his links with City, turning out for them again in September 1991.

Goalkeeper Paul Cooper cost City £20,000 when he signed from Leicester, his League debut occurring on 27th March 1989. This stand-in for Andy Dibble had previously represented Birmingham and Ipswich.

Examples of new players 1988/89

	Previous Club	Date Signed
Trevor Morley	Northampton Town	20th January 1988
Andy Dibble	Luton Town	8th June 1988
Brian Gayle	Wimbledon	9th June 1988
Nigel Gleghorn	Ipswich Town	11th July 1988
Carl Bradshaw	Sheffield Wednesday	29th Sept 1988
Paul Cooper	Leicester City	21st March 1989

Division One Again

The fans waited to see if the new manager, Machin, could take the Blues back to Division One. They were hoping for the big time again, knowing that their club really should be playing teams other than Barnsley, Hull and Shrewsbury from Division Two.

They still turned up at Maine Road in reasonably large numbers. For instance, on August 29th, 1988 a crowd of 22,600 saw the Blues defeated by Oldham Athletic, 4-1. A couple of games later just over 23,000 attended a 1-1 draw with Leeds.

Moments to Remember

The fans were quietly confident that their team would make it to Division One, particularly since the Blues went to the top of Division Two on December 10th, having crushed Bradford City 4-0.

The last few games of the season ended in nail-biting draws. The Oxford United game on April 29th saw City 2-0 down at half time, but the incredible Manchester side had the opposition's net billowing as they went on to win 4-2, once they had recovered their composure.

Above: Steve Redmond, wearing a number 6 shirt, is pictured here during the F.A. Cup tie at Blackpool in 1988. Steve was voted 'Player of the Year' in 1987/88 by City fans.

Manchester City

Moments to Remember

Everyone was on tenterhooks for the final three games which ended in draws:

Date	Opponents	Result	Scorers
May 1st	Crystal Palace	1-1	Gleghorn
May 6th	Bournemouth	3-3	Moulden (2); Morley
May 13th	Bradford City	1-1	Morley

For the last League match of May 1989, City needed just one point for promotion to Division One. Bradford City were one goal up in the first half-hour, with promotion rivals Crystal Palace already 4-0 ahead in their game.

The Manchester fans urged on their side but it looked hopeless as the final whistle approached. Some dejected supporters had begun to leave before the end of the match.

However, City hung on defiantly, and suddenly Morley found the equaliser. The Maine Road side would be going up to Division One!

Top of Division Two 1988/89	
	Points
Chelsea	99
Manchester City	82
Crystal Palace	81

Banana Mania

Unlike the previous season, when City reached the Quarter-finals of both the Littlewoods Cup and FA Cup, the Blues played only two matches in the 1988/9 contest.

The defeat by Third Division Brentford dismayed City followers, but there was some consolation from the Third Round victory against Leicester. This game was reminiscent of a match with this club some 20 years earlier when a Neil Young goal made it 1-0 in the Wembley FA Cup Final.

FA Cup 1988/89				
Date	Round	Opponents	Result	Scorers
Jan 7th	Third Round	Leicester City	1-0	McNab (Penalty)
Jan 28th	Fourth Round	Brentford	1-3	Gleghorn

The Littlewoods Cup had little to offer in terms of thrilling soccer, the Second Round entailing two matches with Plymouth Argyle, with City winning 1-0 in the first leg. The only highlight was the second leg when City blasted in six goals. The opposition defence reeled under a cascade of scheming attacks as the Manchester team won 7-3 on aggregate.

On to Round Three, where the Blues triumphed 4-2 over Sheffield United. An early David White goal gave the fans some hope in the next round when Kenilworth Road was the venue for a tie with Luton

Opposite: Gary Megson (right) transferred to Maine Road from Sheffield Wednesday in January 1989.

Next Pages: May 13th, 1989, and Second Division City require a point at Bradford to guarantee promotion to Division One. Morley scores in the closing minutes and City are back in the big time!

September 23rd, 1989. The Blues' seventh League game of the season was against United. City came out victors with the scoreline at 5-1. One of their goals was scored by Bishop, whose flying header is shown here.

Manchester City

Moments to Remember

Opposite: Peter Reid signed for City on December 12th, 1989, making his debut against Everton four days later.

Town. City could not hold on to their advantage and went out of the competition, losing 1-3.

Do you remember those large inflatable bananas which appeared on the Maine Road terraces as City battled to reach Division One in 1988/9? It is hard to trace the origins of the craze, but it seemed to do the trick as the club eventually made it into Division One at the close of the 1989 season.

Division One Once More

The 1990s brought Division One soccer to Maine Road as fans hoped for more consistent effort from a club which had been relegated in 1983 and 1987.

The first Division One game of 1989/90 was with Liverpool when, understandably, a newly promoted side went down 1-3 to the mighty Merseysiders.

Then came a defeat against Southampton, while a 1-1 draw with Spurs was followed by a defeat at the hands of Coventry City. Queens Park Rangers were beaten, but the Blues then lost away to Wimbledon.

The next game was the Manchester derby which had not been staged for a couple of years because of teams playing in different divisions.

It was impossible to predict the outcome of the game, but once again City surprised everyone. A devastating 5-1 win over the Reds rocked Old Trafford as City soared ahead thanks to well-fashioned goals by Andy Hinchcliffe, Ian Bishop, Trevor Morley and David Oldfield (2).

In the return match of February 3rd, just over 40,000 spectators witnessed a 1-1 result when Brightwell's name appeared on the City scoresheet.

Following the September 1989 fixture with Manchester United, the Blues beat Luton Town 3-1 before going down 4-0 to Arsenal and 2-0 to Aston Villa.

The see-saw results continued with a Clive Allen goal making it 1-1 at Chelsea while Crystal Palace were sent packing in a 3-0 victory. Then there was a 6-0 defeat by Derby – the biggest in the Blues' history for almost 30 years.

Nottingham Forest handed out a 3-0 punishment at Maine Road on November 18th, 1989 while Charlton Athletic held City to a 1-1 draw.

Kendall in charge

November 1989 was a cheerless time with City moving towards relegation. The board took away Mel Machin's managerial role, and old boys Ken Barnes and Tony Book ran the team on a temporary basis until the arrival of new boss Howard Kendall. Early December brought defeat at the hands of Liverpool and Southampton, while the game with Everton resulted in a goalless draw.

Kendall's brief was simple – keep City in Division One. This was hard in the 20 or so League games remaining in 1989/90. In the meantime, life went on at Maine Road, 1989

Moments to Remember

closing with victories over Norwich City and Millwall on December 26th and 30th.

In an effort to carry out the task allotted to him, Howard Kendall introduced some of his former Everton colleagues. Mick Heaton became assistant manager in February 1990 while debut games were played by sweeper Alan Harper and player-coach Peter Reid on 16th December, 1989. Both men had at one stage served with Everton, and interestingly, their first game for City was against Kendall's old side.

Things improved in January and February 1990 following a New Year's Day defeat by Sheffield Wednesday (2-0). The Blues drew against Spurs, defeated Coventry (1-0) and then held Manchester United to a 1-1 draw on February 3rd.

The same score was the outcome of the Wimbledon game, but then Charlton Athletic notched up a victory against City in February. March 1990 witnessed City go down 1-0 to Nottingham Forest followed by three 1-1 draws against Arsenal, Luton Town and Chelsea.

The following month brought victories over Aston Villa, Q.P.R., Sheffield Wednesday, Norwich and Everton. April also saw a 1-1 draw against Millwall plus a 1-0 defeat by Derby County.

Howard Kendall was urging on his squad. In the final League game at Crystal Palace, the Blues were at one stage losing 2-0, but Quinn and Allen made it a 2-2 draw.

So, City stayed in Division One, emerging fourteenth at the end of the season.

	League Division One 1989/90	
		Points
1	Liverpool	79
2	Aston Villa	70
3	Tottenham Hotspur	63
4	Arsenal	62
5	Chelsea	60
6	Everton	59
7	Southampton	55
8	Wimbledon	55
9	Nottingham Forest	54
10	Norwich City	53
11	Q. P. R.	50
12	Coventry City	49
13	Manchester United	48
14	**MANCHESTER CITY**	**48**
15	Crystal Palace	48
16	Derby County	46
17	Luton Town	43
18	Sheffield Wednesday	43
19	Charlton Athletic	30
20	Millwall	26

Millwall Memories

The 1989/90 FA Cup programme was haunted by the spectre of Millwall. The London club had been defeated 2-0 in a League game a week or so before the FA Cup tie, so both City and the fans were confident that a positive result would follow.

Moments to Remember

FA Cup Third Round, 6th January 1990

City – 0   Millwall – 0

Some 25,000 people watched a City squad which included Ashley Ward who was enjoying his first home match with the Blues.

The powerful Scot, Colin Hendry, had made his first City League appearance on November 18th 1989, and this outing against Millwall was his initial F.A. Cup game.

The outcome was a 0-0 draw that needed a replay three days later.

FA Cup Third Round Replay, 9th January 1990

Millwall – 1   City – 1

Relegation-threatened Millwall did not give in at their ground, The Den, and the 90 minute whistle brought a 1-1 draw with City's contribution coming from a Hendry header. Extra time did not resolve the situation and so another replay was on the cards.

FA Cup Third Round, Second Replay, 15th January 1990

Millwall – 3   City – 1

Once again the City faithful had to travel south to The Den where they winced at a couple of Millwall goals in the first 10 minutes. Paul Lake scored for City in the second half, and the Blues' fans prayed for a victory. Unfortunately, a Sheringham effort made it 3-1 for the Londoners and City were out of the FA Cup.

Littlewoods Cup

City tackled Brentford, Norwich City and Coventry City in the Littlewoods Cup of 1989/90. Fans know only too well that Brentford had smashed City's F.A. Cup hopes in January 1989, pushing the Blues out of the competition in Round Four.

A small crowd of only 6,000 saw Brentford once again come out on top as City went down 2-1 in the first leg of Round Two. However, the Manchester club ensured they reached Round Three by defeating Brentford 4-1 in the second leg.

Littlewoods Cup 1989/90

Round	Date	Opponents	Result	Scorer
Two (First Leg)	19th Sept	Brentford	1-2	Oldfield
Two (Second Leg)	9th October	Brentford	4-1	Morley (2); White; Oldfield
Three	25th October	Norwich City	3-1	White; Bishop; Allen
Four	22nd November	Coventry City	0-1	

Manager Machin's old club Norwich City were next on the list, going down 3-1 to the Blues on October 25th.

Sadly, Coventry City forced the Blues out of the Littlewoods Cup on November 22nd with their 1-0 victory.

New Signings

As an example of a typical first team line up in 1989/90, this is the squad which played Crystal Palace in the last League game on May 5th:

Dibble, Brightwell, Harper, Reid, Hendry, Redmond, White, Ward, Heath, Quinn, Lake

Substitutes: Hinchcliffe and Allen

It is interesting to note some of the City old boys who were supporting manager Howard Kendall around this time. Colin Bell was Youth Team Coach, assisted by Glynn Pardoe who also had responsibility for the Reserves. Ken Barnes acted as Chief Scout, while long-serving Tony Book was Youth Development Office.

Clive Allen

Clive Allen was signed from Bordeaux on Bastille Day, the French national holiday, July 14th, 1989. City paid £1 million for an exceptionally talented star whose goal scoring history made the fee seem worthwhile. For instance, while with Spurs, Clive put away 60 goals in just over 100 League games.

His debut match for the Blues was on August 19th, 1989, Clive's first goal appearing in the 1-0 defeat of Queens Park Rangers on September 9th, 1989.

The City crowds soon warmed to London-born Allen whose name appeared on the scoresheets 11 times in 1989/90.

Peter Reid

Peter Reid was 33 when he came to Maine Road on a free transfer from Queen's Park Rangers. He had earlier served with Bolton Wanderers and Everton, having won 13 international caps. He also represented his country in the 1986 World Cup Series.

A former player at Goodison Park under Howard Kendall, Peter was appointed as player-coach at Maine Road. He played his first game for the Blues against former club Everton on December 17th, 1989.

In the 1991/92 season Peter acted as player-manager and has contributed much to the club's recent success.

Niall Quinn

In the game with Chelsea on March 24th, 1990, Niall made his debut for the Blues and scored with a powerful header to give City a share of the points in a 1-1 draw. Born in 1966, Dubliner Niall Quinn, has a tremendous pedigree, representing Eire in the World Cup.

Colin Hendry

This fiery Scot played his initial game with City on November 18th, 1989 against Not-

Moments to Remember

Left: Dublin born Niall Quinn (right) signed from Arsenal on March 15th, 1990 for £800,000.

tingham Forest. The tough, resilient central defender's career had already taken in a couple of clubs – Dundee and Blackburn Rovers.

Fans hoped his £700,000 price tag would pay dividends at Maine Road, and they did not have to wait long for Colin to prove his worth. In the January 13th, 1990 fixture with Spurs he scored in a 1-1 game with his first goal for City. The February meeting with Wimbledon saw the Scot's name on the score sheet in another 1-1 result, while City's 3-1 victory over Q.P.R. in April was again assisted by a Hendry goal.

F.A. Cup games too benefitted from Colin's presence as he scored the Blues' only goal in a 1-1 Millwall tie on January 9th, 1990. Not surprisingly he was voted 'Player of the Year' at Maine Road in 1989/90.

In 1991/92 Hendry only started one match when he put away both City's goals in the 3-2 fixture with Sheffield Wednesday in the Zenith Data Systems Cup Tie.

Coming on regularly as substitute in 1991/92, he was always popular with club and fans. But just two years after his arrival at Maine Road, in November 1991 he agreed terms with Blackburn Rovers.

Interestingly, the £700,000 fee received by the Blues was the sum paid by Maine Road to Blackburn when Colin transferred to City in November 1989.

Summer Arrivals

Mark Brennan, Tony Coton and Neil Pointon signed for City in July 1990. This last player came from Everton in a transfer deal involving Andy Hinchcliffe who moved to the Merseyside club.

Tony Coton left Watford on payment of a £1 million fee by City. Born in Staffordshire in 1961, he made his Blues debut on August 25th, 1990.

The Maine Road club paid Middlesbrough £400,000 for Mark Brennan, who signed on the dotted line in July 1990.

This midfield player had at one stage been on Ipswich Town's books, a club for whom he made almost 170 appearances. Rossendale-born Brennan had gained several England Under-21 caps before moving to Maine Road.

Examples of new signings 1989-91

Name	Date Signed	From
Gary Megson	11th January, 1989	Sheffield Wednesday
Colin Hendry	10th November, 1989	Blackburn Rovers
Peter Reid	12th December, 1989	Queen's Park Rangers
Alan Harper	13th December, 1989	Sheffield Wednesday
Adrian Heath	20th February, 1990	Aston Villa
Niall Quinn	15th March, 1991	Arsenal

8

The Early Nineties

Early Success

The start of a new season was tinged with sadness as fans and club paid homage to Joe Mercer who died on August 9th, 1990.

City had overcome any relegation threats they had faced in February and March 1990, and now supporters eagerly awaited the first League game of the new season on August 25th. This Spurs match was particularly important for defender Neil Pointon and goalie Tony Coton, both of whom were making their first appearances for the Blues.

Although the fans saw their team go down 3-1 to the Londoners, they enjoyed Niall Quinn's first goal of the season.

City then produced some favourable results, beating Everton (1-0) and Aston Villa (2-1), as Peter Reid's presence clearly held together his team's attacking line. The Blues seemed to have discovered the key to consistent soccer, as a 1-1 result with Sheffield United was followed by a 2-1 victory over Norwich City. City's performance demonstrated the side could display a competitive edge when in the mood.

On September 22nd, Mark Ward fired in his second penalty of the season in a 1-1 draw with Chelsea.

City had apparently mastered the technique of unhinging opposition defences, as a 1-1 draw with Wimbledon was followed by a 2-0 victory over Coventry on October 6th. The Blues exposed the limitations of the Midlands side, with Harper and Quinn providing the winners.

The Derby County fixture ended 1-1 as Ward poached another penalty. It was then time for the United -v- City confrontation of October 27th. Two goals by David White and a Colin Hendry contribution had given City what looked like an unassailable 3-1 lead, but then United put away a couple more goals to make it 3-3 at the 90-minute whistle.

Kendall Goes

The November 3rd game with Sunderland finished in a 1-1 draw, and then Howard Kendall surprised everyone by returning to Everton to manage his old club. Fans and the soccer media looked on with interest as Peter Reid was nominated as City's new manager.

In the next game, City went down 2-3 to Leeds with the Blues' goals coming from White and Ward who scored from a penalty.

The Luton Town fixture finished in a 2-2 draw on November 17th, while the Liverpool meeting also resulted in this score, as Quinn squeezed in an equaliser towards the end.

Manchester City

The first two games of December saw City beat Q.P.R. and Spurs, 2-1. The impressive Niall Quinn was there again on December 1st when he put away both goals against Rangers in a wonderfully entertaining match.

On December 22nd, player-manager Peter Reid suffered his first defeat since becoming boss at Maine Road, when the Blues could not match Steve Coppell's Crystal Palace squad who won 2-0.

There then followed a defeat at the hands of Southampton (1-2). The Nottingham Forest win (3-1) on December 29th was made possible by the 'Mighty Quinn' who put a couple over the line, while Clarke secured the other goal to beat Forest.

New Year 1991

A crowd of 30,500 turned out at Maine Road on a cold January 1st to watch a 1-0 win by Arsenal. The "Gunners" were anxious to beat Liverpool in the title race, and they moved one step closer 13 minutes into the second half of the City game. Alan Smith's close range shot found its way into the roof of the net, and the Londoners won by a single goal.

By January 2nd, City were seventh in Division One, a couple of places behind arch-rivals United.

On January 13th a 2-0 Everton victory brought the Blues' fourth defeat in five games. A crowd of 22,000 saw some spectacular saves by Tony Coton in the

Top of Division One, January 2nd, 1991							
	P	W	D	L	F	A	Pts
Liverpool	20	15	3	2	41	16	48
Arsenal	21	14	7	0	41	10	47
C. Palace	21	12	6	3	31	20	42
Leeds	21	11	6	4	36	21	39
Man Utd	21	10	6	5	32	23	35
Tottenham	21	9	6	6	34	27	33
Man City	20	7	8	5	30	28	29

Merseyside encounter, but still Beagrie and Sheedy managed to put a couple past him.

The City squad for this game was

Coton, Brightwell, Pointon, Reid, Hendry, Redmond, White, Heath, Quinn, Megson, Ward

Substitutes: Allen, Harper

The defeat at the hands of Everton was especially poignant for those connected with City, since it was Howard Kendall's 'new' club which had inflicted this blow.

Operation for Reid

Following the game at Goodison Park, player-manager Reid had an operation on January 22nd, but not before he had played a starring role in a 2-0 home victory over Sheffield United even though the player-manager was declared fit only just before the kick-off.

Goals came courtesy of Ward in the 20th and 88th minutes in a game where City were

Opposite: David White has just scored for City in the October 1990 clash with Manchester United. He notched up two goals, while Colin Hendry secured the other in a game which ended 3-3.

119

driven on by the irrepressible Reid. City were now eighth in Division One with 32 points.

When the Blues went to Norwich on February 2nd, they were feeling confident, having won three successive games. On top of this, it was a decade since the Blues had lost to Norwich.

First half goals by Niall Quinn and David White crushed the opponents' morale as the final score read 2-1 for the Maine Road side. Clearly the Quinn-White combination was working at a time when boss Peter Reid was recovering from his knee problems. Early February saw the popular boss playing against Bury, which meant his injury was on the mend. Everyone hoped, of course, that Peter would be in good shape for the FA Cup tie with Notts County on 16th February.

City pulled off an easy 2-1 victory over Chelsea on February 9th. This was a convincing win since, in their previous seven visits to Maine Road, Chelsea had enjoyed six wins and a draw.

Aerial maestro Niall Quinn headed down an Ian Brightwell pass for Gary Megson to score his first goal in more than two years. This 14-minute effort was followed by a David White goal seven minutes later. Chelsea's consolation goal came in the sixty-eighth minute when Wise put away his tenth of the season.

Reid Returns

March heralded considerable promise for City as player-manager Reid returned to his midfield role for the Q.P.R. fixture on March 2nd.

Although the match finished in a 1-0 Q.P.R. victory, there were a couple of near misses for City. Substitutes Allen and Harper replaced Reid and Ward, and a fierce volley by Allen was saved by Rangers' 'keeper.

A victory against Luton Town would place the Blues fifth in Division One, and on March 5th 1991 Quinn scored two of the goals in the 3-0 victory, Allen finding the other. Even though Reid had to limp off with a calf injury in the second half, this did not detract from a dazzling City display. Quinn's contributions came in the twentieth and forty-first minute with Clive Allen's penalty shot crashing into the net 33 minutes into the game. Niall's total number of goals for the season was now an impressive 14.

This victory put the Blues one place ahead of rivals United, as can be seen from the table on the next page.

Qualifying for Europe

Fans and club alike were eager to see City finish in the top three of Division One, and consequently have a chance of qualifying for European soccer in 1991/92.

If Liverpool hung on to their top place in Division One, they would automatically go

Moments to Remember

Top of Division One, March 6th, 1991							
	P	W	D	L	F	A	Pts
Arsenal	26	17	8	1	48	12	57
Liverpool	26	16	6	4	47	23	54
C. Palace	27	14	7	6	35	30	49
Leeds Utd	25	12	7	6	38	26	43
Man City	26	11	8	7	39	33	41
Man Utd	26	11	8	7	38	29	40
Wimbledon	27	10	10	7	41	34	40

into Europe. So too would Arsenal if they won the FA Cup.

City were in a strange position. If they beat the Merseyside team, they would be helping Arsenal to become champions. But to earn a U.E.F.A. place, the Blues would have to overtake the Anfield club.

The upshot of the Maine Road meeting on March 9th was a 3-0 Liverpool victory. This was their first win since Kenny Dalglish's departure, and they conquered City for the tenth time in 11 games at Maine Road.

Two controversial penalties will remain in the minds of those who were cheering on City in a 35,000 crowd. As if to further anger the Manchester fans, they occurred within five minutes of each other.

Hill's Debut

By now, 26-year old full back Andy Hill was approaching the end of a three-month loan period from Bury. He replaced Neil Pointon who began a three- match ban, while Gary Megson was out of the Wimbledon clash on March 16th because of a hamstring injury.

City were urged on in the Wimbledon game when a Fashanu header put the visitors ahead. Then, within a minute, Blues' Mark Ward equalised from the penalty spot, and the 21,000 crowd were left with a 1-1 draw.

In the 23rd March meeting with Coventry an Allen effort produced City's only goal in a 3-1 defeat. City went to Coventry minus defender Colin Hendry, Neil Pointon and newcomer Andy Hill. The Blues put Alan Harper in a sweeper's position, but City had to reshuffle players as Coventry began some aggressive soccer.

City's remaining games of the season included meetings with four of the six teams placed above them – Crystal Palace, Leeds United, Arsenal and Manchester United.

All had vested interests in Europe, a Cup, or the Championship, so City had a few tough battles ahead.

Half a dozen goals in the second half of a March 30th fixture suddenly brought the game to life as Southampton earned a vital point in the battle against relegation.

Ironically, the man who scored Southampton's third goal in the 3-3 draw, just two minutes into injury time, was a former City fan. Alan McLoughlin had lived in Fallowfield, close to Maine Road, where he went to

Next Pages: In the 1990/91 season, Steve Redmond made a total of 46 appearances for City.

Neil Pointon was signed in July 1990 in a deal which included a £400,000 fee, plus the move of Andy Hinchcliffe to Everton.

121

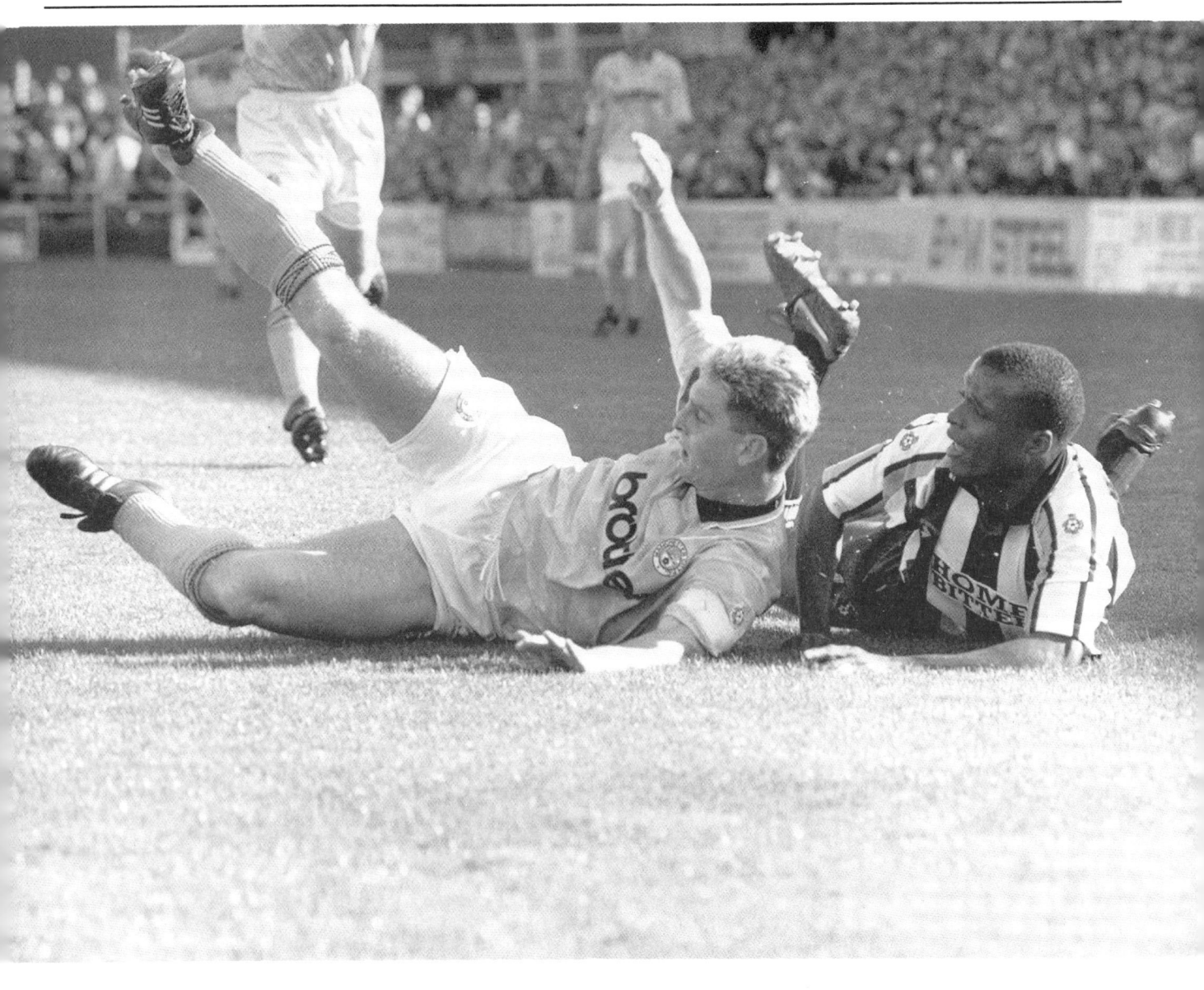

Manchester City

Moments to Remember

watch the Blues in the days of Barnes, Tueart and Hartford. He served a three-year apprenticeship with Manchester United, before moving to Swindon and then Southampton.

Injuries and Suspension Problems

About this time City's strength had been sapped by suspensions, illness and injuries. For example, Neil Pointon returned for the Crystal Palace game on April 1st following a three-match ban. Meanwhile Gary Megson and Andy Hill were forced out through injury, while Colin Hendry's virus infection had kept him out of the squad.

Quinn was at the forefront of the action yet again, his Selhurst Park hat-trick destroying a high-flying Crystal Palace. Niall crushed the opposition with two first half goals in the space of 90 seconds, the third coming in the fifty-fourth minute. The goals brought the Dublin born striker's tally for the season to 22, of which five were scored in internationals.

Salako provided Steve Coppell's side with their only goal in the resounding 3-1 victory for City.

Early April posed a number of problems for manager Peter Reid as injuries forced him to switch David White, Mark Brennan and Ian Brightwell to new positions. Colin Hendry was making a slow come back via Central League games.

Fans and management alike were hoping for a victory against Nottingham Forest, and this encounter on April 6th saw City come out on top, 3-1.

Top of Division One, April 2nd, 1991	
	Pts
Arsenal	65
Liverpool	63
C. Palace	58
Leeds Utd	49
Man. Utd	48
Man. City	46
Wimbledon	45
Tottenham	42

Leeds and Arsenal

The Blues took on Leeds with full back Neil Pointon fully recovered after damaging his ribs during the Forest fixture. With Colin Hendry back in the side after illness forced him to miss four League games, City followers pinned their hopes on a successful outing for the Blues.

The subsequent triumph over Leeds (2-1) plus that earlier defeat of Crystal Palace put City in a strong position when they took on Arsenal, who had been trying for the 'Double'. The FA Cup defeat at the hands of Spurs meant the Gunners now only had the League Championship in their sights.

An interesting aspect of the Arsenal game was that two of England's top goalkeepers were at opposite ends of the pitch. David Seaman was keen to show Graham Taylor that he could match City's Tony Coton, who was equally keen to gain international status.

With a 2-2 final score, City could now boast an impressive five-match run without a defeat. Colin Hendry was not in the starting line-up and, like Peter Reid, he sat on the substitute's bench.

Quinn Saves Penalty!

City's next game was with relegation-threatened Derby County, for whom a defeat would mean Second Division soccer in 1991/92. A win for the Blues could threaten neighbours United if City extended their unbeaten run to six games.

The Derby encounter proved to be a fruitful meeting, as City won 2-1, gaining 14 points from a possible 18 in six unbeaten games.

What a match to remember! Doomed to play Division Two soccer the following season because of Quinn and White goals, Derby must have wondered why they could not beat a team whose goalkeeper, Coton, had been sent off, for dragging down Dean Saunders.

Into the nets came Niall Quinn. Who can ever forget this eventful match when the Irishman kept out a penalty at one end and scored at the other? He made history with the twenty-first minute half-volley and saving of Dean Saunders' penalty.

Three games remained. Could City finish the season in the highest position since 1978 when they also occupied fourth place? Then, Manchester United were tenth, on 42 points.

Here is a reminder of how things looked at that time:

	Top of Division One, 1977/78						
	P	W	D	L	F	A	Pts
Notts. Forest	42	25	14	3	69	24	64
Liverpool	42	24	9	9	65	34	57
Everton	42	22	11	9	76	45	55
Man. City	42	20	12	10	74	51	52
Arsenal	42	21	10	11	60	37	52

Fine Away Victory

The Blues crushed Aston Villa 5-1 with the magnificent David White putting away four goals, while Brennan's contribution came in the sixty-first minute.

This was the Blues' best away First Division win since October 10th, 1959, when they trounced Preston 5-1.

Local Derby

19-year old Martyn Margetson replaced Tony Coton in nets, as the latter began a three-match ban. This was how the first five teams were placed on the morning of Saturday, May 4th – "derby" day:

Top of Division One, before the Derby game on May 4th, 1991							
	P	W	D	L	F	A	Pts
Arsenal	35	22	12	1	65	16	76
Liverpool	35	22	7	6	72	34	73
C. Palace	36	18	9	9	44	41	63
Man. City	36	16	11	9	61	60	59
Leeds	35	17	7	11	55	40	58

The Blues' side comprised:

Margetson, Hill, Pointon, Heath, Hendry, Redmond, White, Brennan, Quinn, Harper, Ward

Substitutes: Reid, Clarke

Unfortunately, City went down 1-0 to United, but there was some consolation for the Maine Road faithful. Their voices were heard when they voted Niall Quinn Manchester City's 'Player of the Year'. The 20-goal marksman had contributed so much to the club over the season, that the award brought little surprise.

Last Game of 1991

On May 11th, 1991, City faced relegation-threatened Sunderland. The Wearsiders went down 3-2 with goals from Quinn (11th, 44th minutes) and White (90th minute).

City produced a cliff-hanger finish in the last minute, as the biggest crowd of the season watched anxiously (39,194). The win allowed City to finish the year in style, coming fifth in Division One:

	Division One at the end of the 1990/91 season
	Pts
Arsenal	83
Liverpool	76
Crystal Palace	69
Leeds	64
MANCHESTER CITY	**62**
Manchester Utd	58
Wimbledon	56
Notts Forest	54
Everton	51
Chelsea	49
Tottenham	48
Q.P.R.	46
Sheffield Utd	46
Southampton	45
Norwich	45
Coventry	44
Aston Villa	41
Luton	37
Sunderland	34
Derby County	24

Moments to Remember

	Opponents	Result		Scorers
A	Tottenham Hotspur	L	1-3	Quinn
H	Everton	W	1-0	Heath
H	Aston Villa	W	2-1	Ward, Pointon
A	Sheffield United	D	1-1	White
H	Norwich City	W	2-1	Quinn, Brennan
A	Chelsea	D	1-1	Ward
A	Wimbledon	D	1-1	Allen
H	Coventry City	W	2-0	Harper, Quinn
A	Derby County	D	1-1	Ward
H	Manchester United	D	3-3	White(2), Hendry
A	Sunderland	D	1-1	White
H	Leeds United	L	2-3	Ward, White
A	Luton Town	D	2-2	White, Redmond
A	Liverpool	D	2-2	Ward, Quinn
H	Queens Park R.	W	2-1	Quinn(2)
H	Tottenham Hotspur	W	2-1	Redmond, Ward
H	Crystal Palace	L	0-2	
A	Southampton	L	1-2	Quinn
A	Nottingham Forest	W	3-1	Quinn(2), Clarke
H	Arsenal	L	0-1	
A	Everton	L	0-2	
H	Sheffield United	W	2-0	Ward(2)
A	Norwich City	W	2-1	Quinn, White
H	Chelsea	W	2-1	Megson, White
A	Queens Park R.	L	0-1	
H	Luton Town	W	3-0	Quinn(2), Allen
H	Liverpool	L	0-3	
H	Wimbledon	D	1-1	Ward
A	Coventry City	L	1-3	Allen
H	Southampton	D	3-3	Allen, Brennan, White
A	Crystal Palace	W	3-1	Quinn(3)
H	Nottingham Forest	W	3-1	Ward, Quinn, Redmond
A	Leeds United	W	2-1	Hill, Quinn
A	Arsenal	D	2-2	Ward, White
H	Derby County	W	2-1	Quinn, White
A	Aston Villa	W	5-1	White(4), Brennan
A	Manchester United	L	0-1	
H	Sunderland	W	3-2	Quinn(2), White

Left: City's Games in 1990/91. The Blues came a respectable fifth in Division One.

1990/91 Cup Competitions

Rumbelows League Cup

Second Round, First Leg September 26th
Torquay United 0, Manchester City 4

Second Round, Second Leg October 10th
Manchester City 0, Torquay United 0

Third Round October 30th
Manchester City 1, Arsenal 2

Only about 5,500 spectators turned out at Torquay to see the seaside town's team lose 4-0 as the Manchester visitors fully exposed the limitations of a Fourth Division side.

Harper, Hendry, Allen and Beckford goals allowed the Blues to move on to the Second Leg of Round Two on October 10th 1990 with a four-goal lead.

City could not score in the Maine Road tie, but they moved into Round Three following a 0-0 result in front of a home crowd of 12,200.

October 30th brought Arsenal to Maine Road, a team who were later to become League Champions. The "Gunners" displayed their skills in a 2-1 victory where City's consolation goal came from substitute Clive Allen.

Zenith Cup

Once referred to as the Full Members' Cup, the Zenith Cup involved City in three matches. In the Second Round on December 19th, the Blues met Middlesbrough who were duly dismissed 2-1 thanks to goals by White and Quinn. For the Third Round a tiny crowd of 5,100 attended Bramall Lane to witness City defeat Sheffield United 2-0. The Yorkshire club simply could not cope with the deadly finishing of Mark Ward who scored both the goals. In Round Four, Leeds eliminated City 2-0, even the Blues had displayed early signs of confidence and competent soccer.

FA Cup 1990/91

Third Round 6th January
Burnley 0, Manchester City 1

City played all three rounds away from home, the first match resulting in a 1-0 victory at Turf Moor, thanks to a Colin Hendry goal. Even though Niall Quinn was left out through injury, City supporters had every confidence in their team with million pound 'keeper Tony Coton in nets.

Fans and squad alike were now set for Round Four.

Fourth Round 26th January
Port Vale 1, Manchester City 2

Port Vale had a reputation for being a giant killer club when it came to FA Cup ties.

City supporters were waiting with interest to see how former Blues player Darren Beckford would perform. Leaving Maine Road to join Port Vale in 1987, the 23-year old striker had hammered in 46 goals during 124 League matches with Vale.

Another touch of irony was that City's

powerful Niall Quinn had almost signed for Port Vale five years previously. Instead of going to the Potteries, the Irish international signed a deal with Arsenal.

Crucial central defender Colin Hendry missed the Fourth Round tie at Port Vale owing to a virus, while Peter Reid was also unfit following a knee operation.

Niall Quinn skilfully volleyed Pointon's twelfth minute centre into the net, but in the thirty-sixth minute former City player Beckford produced a spectacular equaliser.

City experienced some second-half pressure from the enterprising Second Division side. Then, on came £1 million striker Clive Allen as a replacement for Adrian Heath. Clive's first touch scored the winning goal in the seventieth minute when he nodded the ball home, to make it Manchester City 2, Port Vale 1. This was a particularly poignant moment for Allen who had endured an F.A. defeat on the same ground when he played for Spurs four years earlier.

Fifth Round 16th February
Notts County 1, Manchester City 0

Peter Reid's ambition to guide City to Wembley in his first season was ruined at the Notts County ground.

An injury-time winner from striker Gary Lund ended the Blues' dreams of reaching the Final. County, however, were in the Quarter-finals for the first time in seven years. Credit must go to their goalie Steve Cherry who pulled off a series of spectacular saves which prevented City from scoring.

This was quite a moment for the Nottingham 'keeper, who doubtlessly remembered how City had scored 19 times against him when he played for Plymouth and Walsall. Those five Cup ties were now history as his present club revelled in their victory.

City fans would argue that their team was the better side in the Notts County fixture, with Blues' players hitting the post on four occasions. Perhaps the only consolation was that rivals United also lost an FA Cup match – a Fifth Round tie in which Norwich came out on top, 2-1.

A Cup at Last!

Peter Reid achieved Cup success for City in the Shamrock Trophy on March 18th. The Blues drew 2-2 with Shamrock Rovers in Dublin but won 4-2 in the penalty shoot-out. This allowed reserve goalie Margetson to prove his worth, when he saved two spot kicks.

The disappointing news was that the Blues returned from their success with four injured players – Tony Coton, Andy Hill, Steve Redmond and Alan Harper.

As a consequence, when the Maine Road side met Coventry in a League game on March 23rd, they were still recovering from the injuries sustained in the Dublin match.

THE 1991/92 SEASON

Former City manager, Les McDowall died in August 1991, aged 79. The Maine Road

Manchester City

Right: Keith Curle (right) transferred from Wimbledon on August 6th, 1991, for a reputed fee of £2.5 million. The robust defender was Captain in the 1991/92 season.

centre-half moved to City from Sunderland in 1938, before taking up the player-manager's role at Wrexham, 11 years later.

Les returned to Maine Road as manager on June 1st 1950, staying until May 1963. In his first season he guided City back into Division One. Denis Law was one of his most famous signings, the talented star moving to Maine Road for a then British record fee of £55,000 in March 1960.

Curle Arrives

City began the new season with goalkeeper Martyn Margetson in nets as the suspended Tony Coton watched from the bench. He had one more game to sit out on the side line to complete a three-match ban following his sending off against Derby County.

This is how City lined up in their first League match of the 1991/92 season against Coventry on August 17th, 1991:

Margetson, Hill, Pointon, Reid, Curle, Redmond, White, Brightwell, Megson, Brennan

Substitutes: Heath, Hendry

Quinn cleverly outwitted his Coventry markers, scoring with a superb header, to make it a 1-0 victory for the Blues.

Naturally the £2.5 million signing, Keith Curle, was under close scrutiny. He could push out any one of three players – Steve Redmond, Colin Hendry or Ian Brightwell. Curle made his home debut against Liverpool on August 21st, in front of a 37,000 crowd. The 27-year old City skipper was hoping for a change in the Blues' fortunes, as City had not won at home to Liverpool since December 26th, 1985. There was only one newcomer in the Maine Road side that beat Coventry – Tony Coton returning after suspension.

Excellent efforts by all City's players resulted in a 2-1 victory, putting City second in Division One. Man of the Match was without doubt local lad David White, who scored in the twenty-ninth and sixty-fourth minutes, putting City second in Division One. The Merseyside goal came from McManaman.

(In the last eight matches of the 1990/91 season and the first two of the next, the impressive partnership of White and Quinn snatched an incredible 18 goals.)

City were enjoying the best start to a season since 1982/83.

Top of Division One

Mark Brennan guided City to the top of Division One on August 24th when Crystal Palace lost 3-2 to a confident Maine Road side. Brennan's new role as penalty taker allowed him to score twice from the spot. He made another important contribution to the match when he sent over a perfect centre which White volleyed past 'keeper Martyn.

On Saturday evening, August 24th, the Blues topped Division One at a time when opposing defences had no protection against the imagination and variety of City's attacks.

131

Manchester City

Moments to Remember

Top of Division One, August 24th 1991

	P	W	D	L	F	A	Pts
Man. City	3	3	0	0	6	3	9
Man. Utd.	3	2	1	0	3	0	7
Notts. For.	3	2	0	1	6	2	6
A. Villa	3	2	0	1	6	4	6
Norwich	3	1	2	0	6	4	5
Coventry	3	1	1	1	6	2	4
Oldham	3	1	1	1	6	4	4
Wimbledon	2	1	1	0	4	2	4

But the match against Norwich City on August 28th finished in a 0-0 draw. City striker Niall Quinn missed the clash after being rushed to hospital with an abscess on his jaw. It was Manchester's goalkeeper Tony Coton who rescued the Division One pace setters with some memorable saves. In particular, his full-length dive prevented former Maine Road man, David Phillips, from scoring in the twentieth minute.

Quinn against old club

Niall Quinn's abscess was cured for the Arsenal League game on August 31st, and the hardy Irishman was able to have a crack against his former club. Unfortunately, the reigning League champions found their form to destroy City's hopes of continuing as First Division leaders. Swedish international Anders Limpar was the Gunner's hero, when his outstanding goal 12 minutes from the finish ended City's unbeaten run.

Brightwell scored for the Blues after 30 minutes, with Arsenal's goals coming from Smith (forty-sixth minute) and Limpar (seventy-seventh minute), in this fixture which concluded with a 2-1 advantage for the Londoners.

City were in third place at the start of September 1991.

When City defeated Forest 2-1 on September 4th, it was the Andy Hill header five minutes from time that carried the Blues into second position in the League.

The match started in an exciting manner, continued in the same vein and looked like culminating in a 1-1 draw. However, Hill put a powerful header past goalie Crossley, making it 2-1. This happened just five minutes from the end as many fans were leaving the stadium.

City's goals were supplied by Quinn (thirty-ninth minute), Hill (eighty-fifth minute), while Sheringham's close range effort gave Forest a sixty-five minute goal.

Leeds apply pressure

City played in front of approximately 30,000 as Elland Road was the venue for the Battle of the Roses on September 7th, 1991. Before the game, Leeds were sixth in Division One, City second and Manchester United at the top.

Following their 3-0 defeat of City, Leeds moved up to fourth place just below the Blues who had dropped to third slot.

Opposite: August 21st, 1991. City beat Liverpool 2-1 at Maine Road. Niall Quinn (left) is seen challenging a Merseyside player for the ball.

Manchester City

Right: Leeds are a formidable team to play, especially at Elland Road. Niall Quinn eludes Leeds defender Chris Whyte, in a game where the home team notched up a 3-0 win.

Moments to Remember

Top of Division One, September 8th, 1991	
	Pts
Manchester United	17
Liverpool	13
Manchester City	13
Leeds	12
Chelsea	12

David Batty put home a slick pass from Gordon Strachan in the thirty-fourth minute. He had only scored once for Leeds, and this was in a City match on Boxing Day 1987. Before Batty's effort, Dorigo had crashed in an 18-minute goal, with Leeds' third coming from a Strachan penalty.

September Setbacks

City had their first home defeat since March 9th at the hands of Sheffield Wednesday on September 14th. The Yorkshire club's Paul Williams earned Sheffield their first away win of the season as City went down 0-1.

City were unlucky when a Quinn header was deemed offside, as Sheffield continued to batter away at City's defence. It was only superb goalkeeping by Coton which kept the score 0-1. Unfortunately, he could not prevent the Williams winner.

The two seasoned campaigners, Peter Reid and Trevor Francis, were both player-managers of their respective teams. When Sheffield boss Francis trotted out for the last quarter of an hour, the home fans gave a spontaneous round of applause. Many remembered Trevor's single season at Maine Road as a player in 1981/82.

Against Everton in September, the Merseysiders won 1-0, but the Blues enjoyed a 2-1 victory over West Ham on September 21st, thanks to a Redmond penalty and an 89th minute effort by substitute Hendry.

Dibble Recalled

A week later, local side Oldham beat City 2-1 in a game where Keith Curle and Andy Hill had to quit because of injuries before half time. Goalkeeper Dibble, who was on loan to Bolton, was recalled for this Maine Road game when City's number one choice, Tony Coton, pulled out because of flu.

The talented substitute Allen scored two goals for City in the Notts. County clash at Meadow Lane on October 6th, with Sheron providing the other in the Blues' 3-1 victory.

Niall Quinn's excellent second half goal against Spurs on October 19th earned the Blues their third successive win. This put them in third place in the Division, thanks to Curle's defence and Quinn's attacking style which produced a well-deserved 1-0 victory over Spurs.

The Sheffield Influence

Manchester football on October 26th revolved around the Yorkshire city of Sheffield as Wednesday beat Manchester United 3-2, while City defeated Sheffield United by the same score. The Wednesday success meant that the Old Trafford team was pushed from the top of Division One.

Former City player Brian Gayle was captain

Next Page: A goalmouth tussle in the September 1991 fixture, between City and Sheffield Wednesday, at Maine Road. Wednesday were always a force to reckon with for the remainder of the season.

Manchester City

Moments to Remember

Above: Steve Redmond (number 6) stems off a Notts County attack in the League game of October 6th, 1991. Neil Pointon (number 3) and Peter Reid are also on hand. Sheron's goal and Allen's two led to a City victory, the score being 3-1.

of Sheffield United, and produced a couple of equalising headers in the 33rd and 42nd minutes.

The home team's goals came from Sheron (22nd minute), Quinn (37th minute) and Hughes (77th minute). Northern Ireland's new international, Michael Hughes scored the first senior goal of his career to provide City with a hard-earned victory in a game where the Blues hung on defiantly to win.

November '91

The fixture against Southampton on November 2nd caused some concern for Peter Reid, as Niall Quinn was carried off just after the first quarter of an hour. Naturally, the striker was worried about his place in the Republic of Ireland's game with Turkey, which was just over a week away.

The resounding 3-0 Blues' victory was a fair score in a game where Colin Hendry came on for Niall. Goals were expertly supplied by Quinn (10 minutes), Sheron (47 minutes) and Gittens o.g. (58 minutes).

City -v- United

The scene was set for a classic 'derby' encounter between City and Manchester United on November 16th.

The Reds' followers were eager for their side to retain the top slot, since the last time they had won the Championship was way back in 1967. Six years had elapsed since United had won one of these domestic confrontations at Maine Road.

The last time both clubs were in such a buoyant position was in 1968/69. The Maine Road club then brought home the FA Cup, just before carrying off the Cup Winners' trophy in 1970. United, on the other hand, won the European Cup in 1968 and reached the Semi-final of this competition the following year. But, in November '91, a 0-0 draw was the outcome of the Manchester "derby".

The two teams were as follows:

City: Coton, Hill, Pointon, Reid, Curle, Redmond, White, Heath, Quinn, Brightwell, Hughes

Substitutes: Sheron, Allen

United: Schmeichel, Parker, Irwin, Bruce, Webb, Pallister, Robson, Blackmore, McClair, Hughes, Giggs

Substitutes: Ince, Kanchelskis

To make things worse for United, Leeds enjoyed a home victory, which toppled the Reds from the top of Division One.

Top of Division One, November 17th, 1991

	P	W	D	L	F	A	Pts
Leeds	16	9	6	1	27	12	33
Man. Utd.	15	9	5	1	23	7	32
Man. City	16	9	2	5	22	17	29
Aston Villa	16	8	3	5	22	15	27
C. Palace	15	8	3	4	25	25	27
Arsenal	15	7	4	4	30	20	25
Sheff. Wed.	15	7	4	4	26	18	25
Norwich	16	5	8	3	19	17	23

Hendry Leaves

A struggling Luton took the lead against City on two occasions on November 23rd. The 2-2 game ended in a controversial manner with the Blues' Steve Redmond sent off in injury time for a foul on Brian Stein. The resulting free kick did not produce a goal, and consequently the 'Hatters' slipped to the bottom of Division One.

Curle put one away for City in the 45th minute, while a stunning goal from Quinn a quarter of an hour later salvaged a point for the Manchester club.

Just under 22,500 turned out to see City play Wimbledon on November 30th, but the result was a goalless draw.

Colin Hendry moved to Blackburn Rovers in November 1991. He left the Lancashire club just two years before to play at Maine Road. It was clear that the new Rovers manager, Kenny Dalglish, realised the potential of an experienced Hendry who could help to put Blackburn back into Division One.

December '91

In early December, the talented player, Clive Allen, prepared to leave City. The Blues' £1 million signing completed his move to Chelsea for £350,000. Allen seemed to enjoy his new club, scoring a number of impressive goals in his games with Chelsea. His tally was three goals in just four games, including a couple in one match against Oldham on December 21st.

City's impressive away record was destroyed on December 7th by Aston Villa. Still recovering from the mid-week Rumbelows Cup defeat at Middlesbrough, the Blues had drawn one, and won four of their previous five away League games. City's goal came from White, while Regis, Yorke and Daley ensured an important 1-3 win for Villa.

On December 14th, the Blues managed a 2-2 draw with Q.P.R., in spite of leading 2-0 at half time!

A week later, City confronted Liverpool. The Blues were determined to pull off a victory which would be their first at Anfield since Boxing Day 1981. The return of Peter Reid after an absence of six weeks inspired one of the Blues' best performances for some time. A Dean Saunders strike put the Merseysiders 1-0 up in the ninth minute. However, a flurry of City pressure paid off as David White scored in the 48th and 54th minutes. Just eight minutes from the end, Steve Nicol provided a Liverpool equaliser, giving a final score of 2-2.

McMahon Signs

One player who captured the media's attention was Liverpool's Steve McMahon. It was rumoured that the 30-year old midfielder was poised to move to City. In fact Steve was the Blues' Christmas Eve £900,000 signing, and had his first game on Boxing Day, when City took on Norwich City.

McMahon proved his worth as he bolstered the Manchester midfield in a 2-1 victory over Norwich. Although coming off with a hamstring injury in the 71st minute, the Merseyside signing demonstrated he was clearly going to be a valuable asset.

Next Page: Steve McMahon is shown here foxing a Norwich City defender in the 1991/92 season, just after the Merseysider transferred from Liverpool.

Manchester City

When City faced Arsenal on December 28th 1991 McMahon was still recovering from the hamstring injury sustained in his debut game against Norwich.

In a game where two players on each side were cautioned for fouls, Arsenal's hopes of retaining the Division One title took a beating at Maine Road. In the seventieth minute, the home crowd enjoyed David White's seventh goal for the Blues in six games, and the final score read: Manchester City 1, Arsenal 0.

January 1992

In the Maine Road camp, all eyes were on the January 1st clash with Chelsea. One person who had considerable interest in the tie was a recent signing by the Stamford Bridge club – Clive Allen. The former Maine Road player's early games with Chelsea had already produced some impressive goals.

The New Year's Day fixture featured Andy Dibble in nets for the Blues, standing in for Tony Coton who was suffering from food poisoning. Andy pulled off some spectacular saves in the first half.

When it looked as though 1-0 for Chelsea would appear in the results table, City gave further proof of their resilience. In the last 30 seconds of the match, substitute Mike Sheron hit a ball through a packed penalty area and past 'keeper Beasant. The final 1-1 draw put the Blues fourth in Division One on January 1st.

Determined to pick themselves up after the Ayresome Park FA Cup defeat on January 4th, City faced Steve Coppell's Crystal Palace in a League game one week later.

The outcome of the Selhurst Park fixture was again a 1-1 draw. A contested penalty allowed City to hang on to their place near the leaders. Keith Curle converted the spot kick in the seventy-ninth minute of a fixture where Palace's Bright provided the London team with a forty-third minute goal.

Fans had the chance to savour David White's new role in the Palace game. Switching from winger to striker, it was hoped that the 24-year old City forward could work in tandem with Niall Quinn.

January 18th brought Coventry City to Maine Road just four days after the Midlands team had been knocked out of the F.A. Cup at Cambridge. Many years ago, Coventry had played against City in a Division Two game at Maine Road on November 19th, 1938. The home side achieved a 3-0 victory with goals supplied by Doherty (2) and Herd.

The January 1992 meeting of the two clubs will not be remembered for the same excitement and flair. A rather pedestrian game ended 1-0 in favour of the Maine Road club, thanks to a David White goal. The striker blasted in his 14th of the season from 15 yards past goalkeeper Ogrizovic.

Credit must also go to the Blues' Tony Coton who kept out a six-yard drive from Robert Rosario. The City goalie plucked the ball from the air with one hand, and his efforts allowed the side to retain their lead.

Manchester City

February '92: Championship Challenge carries on

Player-manager Peter Reid and £900,000 signing Steve McMahon guided the Blues to a 1-0 victory over Spurs on February 1st. This result put City in the fourth place of Division One.

Fans from both sides waited with interest to see how former City star Paul Stewart would perform. He occupied a midfield position alongside Tottenham's Vinny Samways.

The last Blues' player to transfer to Spurs was Bill Felton, who moved South in 1932 following a three year spell with City.

The Maine Road club faced a Spurs team on February 1st, 1992, whose League record to date had been six away wins and seven home defeats. The previous October, a White Hart Lane meeting resulted in a 1-0 win for City, thanks to a Quinn goal. However, in the February match, both he and Adrian Heath were out of the squad.

City were inspired by Steve McMahon's fine performance as he laid on a succession of accurate passes to Michael Hughes and David White. It was this second player who provided the twenty-ninth minute winner in a game which ended with a score of 1-0 in favour of the Manchester side.

Quinn Returns

Striker Niall Quinn returned for the February 8th fixture with Sheffield United, following his two match suspension. With this talented player on the team, fans were hoping he would increase the attacking options of a team who were keen to maintain their challenge for a European place. However, City went down 2-4 to Sheffield United in February 1992. The Yorkshire side's Brian Deane scored one goal and set up a couple more. One of these was put away by City old boy Brian Gayle, while Dane Whitehouse scored the other. A further Sheffield goal was a contribution by Mike Lake, whose brother Paul is on City's books.

The Blues' goals came in the form of a Curle penalty and a fierce Hill volley. City were no doubt disappointed to lose, but it was only their second League defeat in 17 games.

In the Top Three

City were determined to move higher up Division One, and this they did in no uncertain manner, starting with a resounding 4-0 victory over Luton on February 15th, 1992. Few clubs could compare with the Blues' outstanding performance in this exciting game.

In the November '91 fixture against Luton, at Kenilworth Road, City came away with a 2-2 draw. On that day Peter Reid had to sit on the substitute's bench, following an injury which was sustained in the earlier City –v- United tussle.

Prior to the latest encounter, there had been a total of 33 League games when each side had won 11, drawn 11 and lost 11; this time, a confident Manchester club produced its

Opposite: Ian Brightwell (left) tackles Coventry's Kenny Sansom in the League game of January 18th, 1992. Cheshire-born Brightwell has played in every outfield position for the Blues.

143

highest-ever home win against Luton with a convincing 4-0 result. David White put two away in the fifteenth and forty-eighth minutes, while Hill and Heath scored a couple of second half goals.

The 1992 encounter finished in a 1-2 victory for Keith Curle's former club, Wimbledon. The London team's John Fashanu, provided his team with a goal, while a forty-four minute header by Earle saw City go into the dressing room 2-0 down at half-time.

Substitute Sheron beat Wimbledon's Seger 15 minutes from the end of a game where only 5,800 turned up to see City win 2-1.

Top of Division One, February 23rd, 1992

	Pts
Manchester United	60
Leeds United	56
Manchester City	50

When City entertained Aston Villa on February 29th, the Blues were out to avenge the December 1991 League fixture, when a 3-1 overthrow of the Blues was City's first defeat in half a dozen games.

But the February '92 match was a different story, thanks to some telling contributions from Steve McMahon. He created both goals in the 2-0 victory, the first of which was volleyed home after just three minutes by Niall Quinn.

In the 75th minute, David White pounced on a McMahon through ball and pushed it past goalie Les Sealey.

March '92

Simpson and Vonk Arrive

A £500,000 fee brought Swindon player Fitzroy Simpson to Maine Road early in March '92. He would work alongside Steve McMahon in midfield, adding strength to this area of City's squad.

A confident City visited Q.P.R.'s stadium on March 7th, knowing that the London club had not won a single game since that 4-1 victory over Manchester United on January 1st. Earlier in the season, the Blues had drawn 2-2 in a League fixture and defeated Rangers 3-2 in a Rumbelows Cup replay, following a goalless draw.

Simpson came on in the sixtieth minute to make his first division debut, but this did not aid the situation: City lost 4-0 to Q.P.R., in their biggest defeat of the season. The Maine Road side had now moved to fourth place in Division One.

Dutchman Michel Vonk also joined City about this time. He had previously played with S.V.V. Dordrecht.

City on TV

The Blues faced Southampton in the televised League match of March 14th. The encounter was witnessed by 24,000 spectators at Maine Road, plus a large T.V. audience. Sadly, the Blues lost narrowly by 0-1, the 36 minute goal being supplied by Southampton's Dowie.

Tough Opposition

In a four week spell after March 21st, City took on some formidable opposition – Notts. Forest, Leeds and Manchester United.

The first of these teams had claimed a victory over the Old Trafford club three days before Forest entertained City on March 21st. This had been Nottingham's third successive League win. Brian Clough's side had been beaten 2-1 at Maine Road in September '91, thanks to the fine efforts of Niall Quinn and Andy Hill. But City's success was not repeated on March 21st 1992, when Rumbelows Cup Finalists, Forest, beat the Blues 0-2.

As March drew to a close, people reflected on City's impressive performance in the previous six months. Starting September in a mid-table position, by October, they had climbed to third place, staying on the heels of the leaders until March.

Injury Problems

As City prepared to meet Chelsea on March 28th, Pointon, Heath, Coton, Quinn and Curle were all receiving some sort of treatment in the week prior to the game. Chelsea had lost their previous three matches, and the Blues had drawn 1-1 with the London club on New Year's Day 1992.

In the March '92 encounter, the score was 0-0. In fairness to City, they did engineer three impressive scoring chances in the first six minutes. However, White was deprived on two occasions, while a McMahon-Brightwell move was stemmed by a brave save on the part of the Chelsea 'keeper, Beasant.

The result of the game meant that City moved to sixth place in Division One. The match demonstrated that Peter Reid had established a formidable midfield trio in Steve McMahon, Ian Brightwell and Fitzroy Simpson. Dutchman Michel Vonk also had his full debut for City in this match.

April '92

The first week of April was a busy time for the Blues, who had faced Leeds United and Manchester United in a 4-day period.

It was also a good period for 'keeper Tony Coton, who had just been awarded the prestigious *First Division Goalkeeper of the Year* Award, from players in the P.F.A.

As far as the Yorkshire club were concerned, from a total of 81 Football League meetings, which went back to 1919, the Blues had won 37, drawn 13 and lost 31 games. City's best home wins had been in 1936, 1938 and 1981. On each occasion, the Maine Road side had won by a 4 goal margin.

Top of Division One – April 1st, 1992

	P	W	D	L	F	A	Pts
Man. Utd.	35	19	13	3	56	25	70
Leeds Utd.	36	18	15	3	65	31	69
Sheff. Wed.	35	17	9	9	54	48	60
Liverpool	35	15	13	7	42	31	58
Arsenal	35	14	13	8	62	41	55
Man. City	35	15	9	11	45	42	54

Next Page: Tony Coton, First Division Goalkeeper of the Year, demonstrating his agility in the 1991/92 season.

Manchester City

Moments to Remember

So what happened on April 4th, 1992? The Maine Road side repeated that impressive scoring record as they crushed Leeds 4-0 once again!

Manchester United 1, City 1

In the 1-1 draw at Old Trafford on April 7th, Ryan Giggs scored for United with a 25 yard left-foot drive past 'keeper Coton.

Just 10 minutes into the second half, Pointon clashed with Giggs and the referee had little option but to dismiss the full back from the field. City fans now wondered how their team could hold off United with only 10 men. The Maine Road side stemmed off various probing attacks by the Reds, but the Blues equalised with a penalty, from Keith Curle which easily beat Peter Schmeichel. This spot kick was awarded after Bruce had brought down White on the edge of the area.

The "derby" teams were as follows:

City: Coton, Hill, Pointon, Brennan, Curle, Vonk, Sheron, Quinn, Simpson, McMahon

Substitutes: I.Brightwell, Reid

United: Schmeichel, Donaghy, Irwin, Bruce, Blackmore, Pallister, Giggs, Ince, McClair, Hughes, Sharpe

Substitutes: Kanchelskis, Phelan

Impressive Tony Coton

On April 11th, City were beaten 0-2 by Sheffield Wednesday. The Blues were now sixth in Division One.

Top of Division One – April 12th, 1992

Team	P	Pts
Leeds United	38	72
Manchester United	36	71
Sheffield Wednesday	38	67
Arsenal	38	64
Liverpool	37	58
Manchester City	38	58

Despite the setback, City were still pressing for a top five place and one consolation from the defeat at Hillsborough was the fine form of 'keeper Tony Coton, who pulled off some spectacular saves. He made a brilliant effort which prevented David Hirst from scoring, and then he saved acrobatically from a Nigel Pearson header. All this reminded everyone why City's 'keeper had been chosen by the First Division Goalkeeper of the year.

Sheffield's first goal was supplied by Hirst in the 56th minute. Later on in the game, a Wednesday move saw Nigel Worthington beat Coton with a ferocious volley in the eighty-eighth minute.

Easter Games, 1992

Easter Saturday and Bank Holiday Monday, saw City face West Ham United and Everton, on April 18th and 20th.

The fixture against the 'Hammers' took place in front of 25,600 spectators, who occupied only three sides of the Maine Road ground. Demolition of the Platt Lane stand had already begun, as work progressed on the redevelopment of this end of the stadium.

Manchester City

Examples of City -v- West Ham games		
Date	Result	Scorers
March 24th, 1962	West Ham 0 City 4	Dobing (3), Hayes
Sept. 8th, 1962	City 1 West Ham 6	Barlow
Aug. 17th, 1974	City 4 West Ham 0	Marsh (2), Tueart Doyle

City had won 2-1 in the September '91 League game thanks to goals by Colin Hendry and Steve Redmond, and earlier confrontations between the two clubs had produced some high-scoring matches.

The crowd had barely settled before City went ahead in the second minute of the game. It was Neil Pointon's first goal in 19 months which gave the Blues such an early lead. He had last scored on September 5th, 1990, against Aston Villa. The seventy-seventh minute saw substitute Wayne Clarke convert a low Mike Sheron cross into a superb goal.

Everton defeated!

Many City fans travelled to Goodison Park on Easter Monday. As they drove down the M62, Blues' followers were no doubt mindful that Everton boss, Howard Kendall, had been manager at Maine Road in 1989/90.

A magnificent City performance resulted in a 1-2 victory – their first away win since early November. A vintage Quinn piece of action lifted City as he put away the first goal after just 70 seconds! This was Niall Quinn's eleventh goal of the season. His twelfth came in the twenty-third minute of the Everton game, and was the culmination of some enterprising play by David White and Mike Sheron. The result placed City fifth in the First Division, some four points behind Arsenal.

Ending the 1991/92 Season

Nearing relegation, Notts County were determined to win against City on April 25th. The Blues, however, were also intent on claiming a victory. This would ensure that City would not finish the season lower than fifth place in Division One.

On the day, the formidable City squad swung into action and produced an emphatic 2-0 victory in the penultimate League match of the season. Simpson and Quinn scored for the Blues in the thirty-third and fifty-fifth minutes. The first goal was a left-foot effort. Niall Quinn's diving header was his 14th goal of the season.

The last League game of the season took place on May 2nd at a time when City had consolidated themselves as one of the leading sides in the country. The Blues visited Oldham Athletic with three convincing wins behind them.

The Boundary Park side were in a confident mood, having defeated opposition in the previous four home Division One games before they met City. However, the May '92 confrontation saw the Manchester club thrash Oldham 2-5. The home side scored first, but this did not deter a confident City.

Youngster Adrian Mike put one away in the sixteenth minute and this sparked a comeback for the Blues.

Ace marksman White nodded in a second goal to give City a useful 2-1 lead at the interval.

Following the break, the Manchester club attacked almost at will. Oldham flinched under the onslaught of a confident City squad, which exuded skill and pace.

David White achieved a hat-trick in this game as his efforts eluded 'keeper Keeley in the sixty-third and sixty-eighth minutes. This gave the striker the impressive tally of 21 goals for the season.

A further City goal was subsequently provided by Mike Sheron.

Poor Oldham must have wondered what hit them as the Manchester club secured three second half goals in under seven minutes!

Former City striker, Paul Moulden, reduced the Blues' lead when he scored 3 minutes from the end to make it 5-2. But this did not detract from a superb performance which was provided by a quality City side.

This was City's fourth successive win, which encouraged fans and the club to confidently look forward to a promising 1992/93 season.

Here is the squad which represented City in this final game of the 1991/92 season:

Coton, Hill, I. Brightwell, Simpson, Curle, Vonk, White, Sheron, Quinn, Mike, McMahon

Substitutes: Redmond, Hughes

This excellent end to the season saw City in an impressive fifth position.

A couple of days after this last match, two City stars received prestigious awards, which reflected their contribution to the club.

Tony Coton was voted City's Player of the Year, while 18-year old striker Adrian Mike was awarded the Young Player of the Year award.

1991/92 Cup Competitions

Rumbelows League Cup 1991/92

Second Round, First Leg, September 25th

City 3, Chester 1

Chester were no match for Manchester City who won 3-1 with goals from White and Quinn (2).

Bennett gave the Third Division side some hope, with a 70th minute equaliser but, in the next 10 minutes, that man Quinn scored twice.

Second Round, Second Leg, October 8th

City 3, Chester 0

The Second Leg saw City hammer Chester once more, and come out with a 6-1 aggregate scoreline, with goals from Allen, Sheron and Brennan.

Third Round, October 29th
City 0, Q.P.R 0

This was a rather dreary performance by the two First Division clubs. The score of 0-0 indicated the lack of scoring chances and the tie went to a replay at Loftus Road.

Third Round Replay, November 20th
Q.P.R. 1, City 3

Penrice gave Rangers an early lead but two goals from Adrian Heath, his first goals for 14 months, and a late strike from Niall Quinn, eased City through to Round Four.

Fourth Round, December 3rd
Middlesbrough 2, City 1

A gloomy first half was dominated by fog in this tie, where the young North East team pushed City out of the Rumbelows Cup.

Substitutes Sheron and Allen replaced Hughes and Brennan. David White supplied City's late goal in the eighty-seventh minute, with Middlesborough's coming in the fifty-sixth and sixty-eighth minutes.

Zenith Cup 1991/92

October 23rd 1991
Sheffield Wednesday 3, City 2

City's Zenith Data Systems Cup Tie at Sheffield Wednesday was plagued by injury problems. Seven senior players had to watch from the sidelines as Wednesday claimed a victory. At one stage City were leading 2-1 thanks to goals by the brilliant Hendry in the twenty-sixth and eighth minutes.

F.A. Cup 1991/92

Several titanic confrontations were promised as the FA Cup draw was announced on December 7th, 1991. Wrexham, for example faced Arsenal, while Middlesbrough entertained Manchester City.

The Maine Road club would face the North East side who had knocked them out of the Rumbelows Cup on December 3rd, 1991. Again, Manchester United were incredibly paired with Leeds United, only a few hours after the two top clubs were drawn against each other in the Rumbelows Cup Quarter finals.

Almost unbelievably they were set to clash twice in the two Cups in the same week! And a League match was scheduled between them just six days before the Cup games!

City went to Ayresome Park on January 4th, 1992 to tackle Middlesbrough in Round Three of the FA Cup. They were fortified by an impressive Christmas period in which they consolidated their League position with two away draws and two home wins.

Fans and players alike were mindful of that 2-1 defeat at the hands of Middlesborough in the Rumbelows Cup on December 3rd. When the FA Cup tie started on January 4th the crowd of 21,000 included some 6,000 City fans.

Steve McMahon was now in the squad having recovered from his injury over the Christmas period. Niall Quinn latched on to

City's Games 1991/92

Date	Opponents	Result	Scorer(s)
August 1991			
17	Coventry City	1-0	Quinn
21	Liverpool	2-1	White (2)
24	Crystal Palace	3-2	Brennan (2 pens), White
28	Norwich City	0-0	
31	Arsenal	1-2	Brightwell
September 1991			
4	Nottingham Forest	2-1	Quinn, Hill
7	Leeds United	0-3	
14	Sheffield Wednesday	0-1	
18	Everton	0-1	
21	West Ham United	2-1	Redmond (pen), Hendry
25	Chester City (R. Cup 2)	3-1	White (2), Quinn
28	Oldham Athletic	1-2	White
October 1991			
6	Notts County	3-1	Sheron, Allen (2) 1 pen
8	Chester City (R. Cup 2)	3-0	Allen, Sheron, Brennan
19	Tottenham Hotspurs	1-0	Quinn
23	Sheffield Wednesday (Z.D.S. Cup)	2-3	Hendry (2)
26	Sheffield United	3-2	Sheron, Quinn, Hughes
29	Queen's Park Rangers (R. Cup 3)	0-0	
November 1991			
2	Southampton	3-0	Quinn, Sheron, own goal
16	Manchester United	0-0	
20	Queen's Park Rangers (R. Cup 3R)	3-1	Heath (2), Quinn
23	Luton Town	2-2	Curie, Quinn
30	Wimbledon	0-0	
December 1991			
3	Middlesborough (R. Cup 4)	1-2	White
7	Aston Villa	1-3	White
14	Queen's Park Rangers	2-2	White, Curle
21	Liverpool	2-2	White (2)
26	Norwich City	2-1	Quinn, White
28	Arsenal	1-0	White
January 1992			
1	Chelsea	1-1	Sheron
4	Middlesborough (F.A. Cup 3)	1-2	Reid
11	Crystal Palace	1-1	Curle (pen)
18	Coventry City	1-0	White
February 1992			
1	Tottenham Hotspurs	1-0	White
8	Sheffield United	2-4	Curle (pen), Hill
15	Luton Town	4-0	White (2), Hill Heath
22	Wimbledon	1-2	Sheron
29	Aston Villa	2-0	Quinn, White
March 1992			
7	Queen's Park Rangers	0-4	
15	Southampton	0-1	
21	Nottingham Forest	0-2	
28	Chelsea	0-0	
April 1992			
4	Leeds United	4-0	Hill, Sheron, Quinn, Brennan
7	Manchester United	1-1	Curle (pen)
11	Sheffield Wednesday	0-2	
18	West Ham United	2-0	Pointon, Clarke
20	Everton	2-1	Quinn (2)
25	Notts County	2-0	Simpson, Quinn
May 1992			
2	Oldham Athletic	2-5	Mike, White (3), Sheron

Z.D.S. Cup – Zenith Data Systems Cup
R. Cup – Rumbelows Cup

Manchester City

a Michael Hughes centre in the 29th minute, permitting Peter Reid to nip past Nicky Mohan. The veteran Blues' boss then cleverly volleyed a delightful shot past Stephen Pears, making it 1-0 for the Manchester side.

McMahon was substituted at half time and City fans were becoming quietly confident that a win was on the cards. Suddenly, however, a replay looked likely. Middlesborough's Alan Kernaghan headed in an 80th-minute equaliser following an impressive corner from Phillips. Then, there was more drama as Wilkinson found another goal for Lennie Lawrence's team just one minute later and the final whistle brought a score of Middlesbrough 2, City 1.

THE 1992/93 SEASON

Flitcroft, Holden and Phelan

Summer, 1993, saw City win two games in Ireland. The Blues defeated Limerick 1-3 in May, and then notched up a 0-3 victory against a League of Ireland XI on July 18th. Unhappily, 'keeper Andy Dibble sustained a broken leg in this second match.

Just before City set off for the July match in Ireland, Niall Quinn signed a five-year contract. The Eire international player had cost City only £800,000 when he transferred from Arsenal in March 1990.

In the close season, Blues' defenders Neil Pointon and Steve Redmond left for Oldham, but winger Rick Holden joined City for £900,000 from Oldham Athletic. Born in 1964, Rick began his soccer career with Burnley before transferring to Halifax Town. Moving to Watford for £125,000 in March 1988, Rick represented this club for 18 months before signing for Oldham Athletic in August 1989.

Born on November 6th, 1972, in Bolton, Garry Flitcroft made his first team debut in a friendly game against Derry City in January 1992. The exciting young player has displayed exceptional ability since breaking through into the first team; he was a substitute for the opening Premier League game against Q.P.R. on August 17th.

Terry Phelan played his first game for the Blues against Norwich City on August 20th, 1992. Salford-born Terry became the most expensive full-back in British soccer. The 25-year-old was signed at £2.5 million from Wimbledon, and had represented the Republic of Ireland Youth 'B' and Under 21 teams. His professional career began with Leeds United for whom he made his debut in 1985. He moved to Swansea City, then joined Wimbledon in a £100,000 deal in July 1987.

Premier League Soccer

City's first Premier League fixture of the 1992/3 season was on August 17th when the Blues held Q.P.R to a 1-1 draw at Maine Road. David White scored the goal, and the line-up at the start of the new season was:

Coton; Hill; I. Brightwell; Simpson; Curle; Vonk; White; Lake; Quinn; Holden; McMahon;

Substitutes: Sheron; Flitcroft.

Opposite: David White was City's leading goalscorer in 1991/92.

Manchester City

Right: Changing places – Steve Redmond, now with Oldham Athletic, challenges "Latics" old boy Rick Holden during the exciting 3-3 draw at Maine Road.

On August 19th, City went down 0-2 away to Middlesborough. Paul Lake was injured after 8 minutes. Niall Quinn was sent off, and he missed games against Sheffield Wednesday, Middlesborough and Chelsea while suspended.

Three days after the encounter with Middlesborough, the Blues lost 0-1 to Blackburn Rovers, but could have salvaged something from the game with better finishing.

The visit of Norwich City to Maine Road on August 25th included a batch of former Manchester City players – Darren Beckford, Gary Megson, David Phillips and the coach, John Deehan. Mark Robins also moved from the North. He played for Manchester United before going to Carrow Road.

Before the August match, Norwich and Manchester City had played 34 League games. The Blues had won 18, drawn 13 and lost only 3. In 1991/92 the Maine Road side had enjoyed a 2-1 victory, and fans were now hoping for another home win. They were not disappointed! A crowd of just over 23,000 saw City emerge victors by a 3-1 scoreline.

David White netted a goal just before half time. Former Blues' star Gary Megson headed in the equaliser in the second half, but David White and Steve McMahon made sure of a victory as they made it 3-1. This was Steve's first goal for a City team since his transfer from Liverpool on Christmas Eve, the previous year. Terry Phelan clearly enjoyed his first game for City and demonstrated some impressive skills.

When Oldham faced the Blues on 29th August, City old boys Steve Redmond and Neil Pointon returned to Maine Road. Home fans were still mindful of the spectacular 5-2 win over "Latics" the previous season; in the August 1992 encounter, a 3-3 result meant that City and Oldham had drawn seven times in 35 League games.

The Blues had won 18 times and had lost 10 matches. The three goals were supplied by Vonk, White and Quinn. In a fast-moving first half we were treated to Niall's first goal of the season and Michel Vonk's initial goal in English soccer.

Brought on as a replacement for Sheron in the 80th minute Garry Flitcroft made his League debut for City as substitute. The young player had his first full game on September 1st when City had a 1-0 away win against Wimbledon. In this fixture, former Wimbledon players Terry Phelan and Keith Curle gave good performances.

The single goal was claimed by David White. No doubt this reinforced England manager Graham Taylor's choice in selecting White in the full England squad to face Spain. Taylor watched the Wimbledon game having also called up Mike Sheron for international duty with the Under-21 side.

City – 3, Sheffield Wednesday – 0

City pulled off an emphatic 3-0 win over Sheffield Wednesday on September 5th with two goals from David White and one from Michel Vonk. This made White the Premier League's top scorer as the Blues enjoyed their first victory at Hillsborough in 22 years.

Moments to Remember

Manchester City

Right: Rising stars Garry Flitcroft and Mike Sheron – both of whom went on to represent England at Under 21 level – in action against Middlesborough in September.

Early in September, several City stars changed their sky blue shirts for international colours. On the 9th of that month David White made his full England debut in Spain, while the Republic of Ireland squad included Niall Quinn and Terry Phelan. The Irish side won 4-0 against Latvia in a game, which was the 32nd time Niall had represented his country.

City were now placed ninth in the Premier League.

City went down 0-1 to Middlesbrough a week after the Sheffield Wednesday fixture. The Manchester side was missing the suspended Niall Quinn, and an unfortunate own goal by Garry Flitcroft gifted the points to the visitors. The narrow victory was the first League win by Middlesboro at Maine Road in 42 years!

Injury problems

The City-v-Chelsea clash was televised on September 20th and once again, City lost by a single goal, scored by Mick Harford. Ironically, the decisive score came when City were reduced to 10 men: Rick Holden was off the pitch for stitches following a collision with Terry Phelan.

In September, several City players required medical attention. Paul Lake travelled to the U.S. for major surgery on his cruciate ligament while Michel Vonk needed an ankle operation. Meanwhile, Steve McMahon's operation relieved trapped nerves in his toe. He made a quick recovery and played in the reserves at Maine Road on September 24th.

The Arsenal League match will be remembered for Tony Coton's brilliant goalkeeping skills. His efforts kept the score to 0-1 at Highbury in a game where Steve McMahon played after injury had kept him out for five matches.

No Matches lost in October

Early in the month, several City players were advised of impending international duties. Mike Sheron was part of the England under-21 squad, while Niall Quinn and Terry Phelan went to Denmark with the Republic of Ireland side.

The Blues lost no Premier League matches this month; they drew against Nottingham Forest and Crystal Palace, and defeated Southampton and Everton.

In the October 3rd 2-2 draw against Forest, Holden and Simpson scored in the 17th and 64th minutes, but Nottingham's Stuart Pearce snatched an equaliser just a few minutes from the end of the game. This was the 23rd draw in the 78 League games between City and Forest. The Blues won 32 games and lost 22.

On October 17th, City drew 0-0 with Crystal Place in front of an away crowd of just over 14,000. The Blues were unlucky not to win at Selhurst Park, and Niall Quinn came close to scoring, particularly when his header from a Rick Holden corner was cleared off the line by goalkeeper Nigel Martyn. This

Moments to Remember

Manchester City

Right: Niall Quinn and Andy Hill battle with four Leeds defenders during City's 4-0 victory over the champions in November.

Palace game is also remembered for Andy Hill's sterling work in defence where he starred as a replacement for the injured Michel Vonk.

The home match against Southampton was on October 24th, when heavy rainfall produced a sodden Maine Road pitch. Niall Quinn was unlucky when a magnificent header hit the bar, but Mike Sheron netted the rebound to rescue the game from stalemate and give City a deserved 1-0 win.

This is how the top half of the Premier League looked after the game against the 'Saints'.

Top of the Premier League, October 28th 1992

TEAM	P	PTS
Blackburn Rovers	13	26
Norwich City	13	26
QPR	13	23
Arsenal	13	23
Coventry City	13	22
Aston Villa	13	21
Manchester United	13	21
Chelsea	13	19
Middlesbrough	13	17
Leeds United	13	17
Ipswich Town	13	17
Manchester City	13	17

City were defeated by Tottenham in the Coca Cola Cup on October 28th, but hopes were high when the Blues travelled to Everton three days later. At Goodison Park, there was a thrilling spectacle as a confident Manchester side earned a well-deserved 3-1 victory.

City clinched the game with goals by White (1) and Sheron (2). The Everton goal was the result of an own goal on the part of Ian Brightwell.

The Everton game was a memorable one for Peter Reid, who played against his old club. It was the stalwart's 500th League appearance. The Blues had not lost a Premier League game since they met Arsenal on September 28th.

City – 4, Leeds United – 0

Having dismissed Everton 3-1, the Maine Road army now set about the overthrow of Leeds United on November 7th, 1992. A resounding 4-0 victory underlined the strength of a rampant Manchester City. The Blues had beaten the Yorkshire side by the same score in April, 1992.

Phelan had a particular interest in the match. Terry started his professional career with Leeds in 1985, leaving them the following year. Only three players from those days were now at Elland Road – Scott Sellars, David Batty and Mervyn Day.

Leeds had had no away wins since they clinched the First Division title at Sheffield United the previous April, while City had registered 38 wins in the 82 League fixtures with Leeds over the years.

This exciting match kicked off on Saturday November 7th 1992 in front of 27,255 spectators. In the 13th minute, Mike Sheron scored his fourth goal in three League

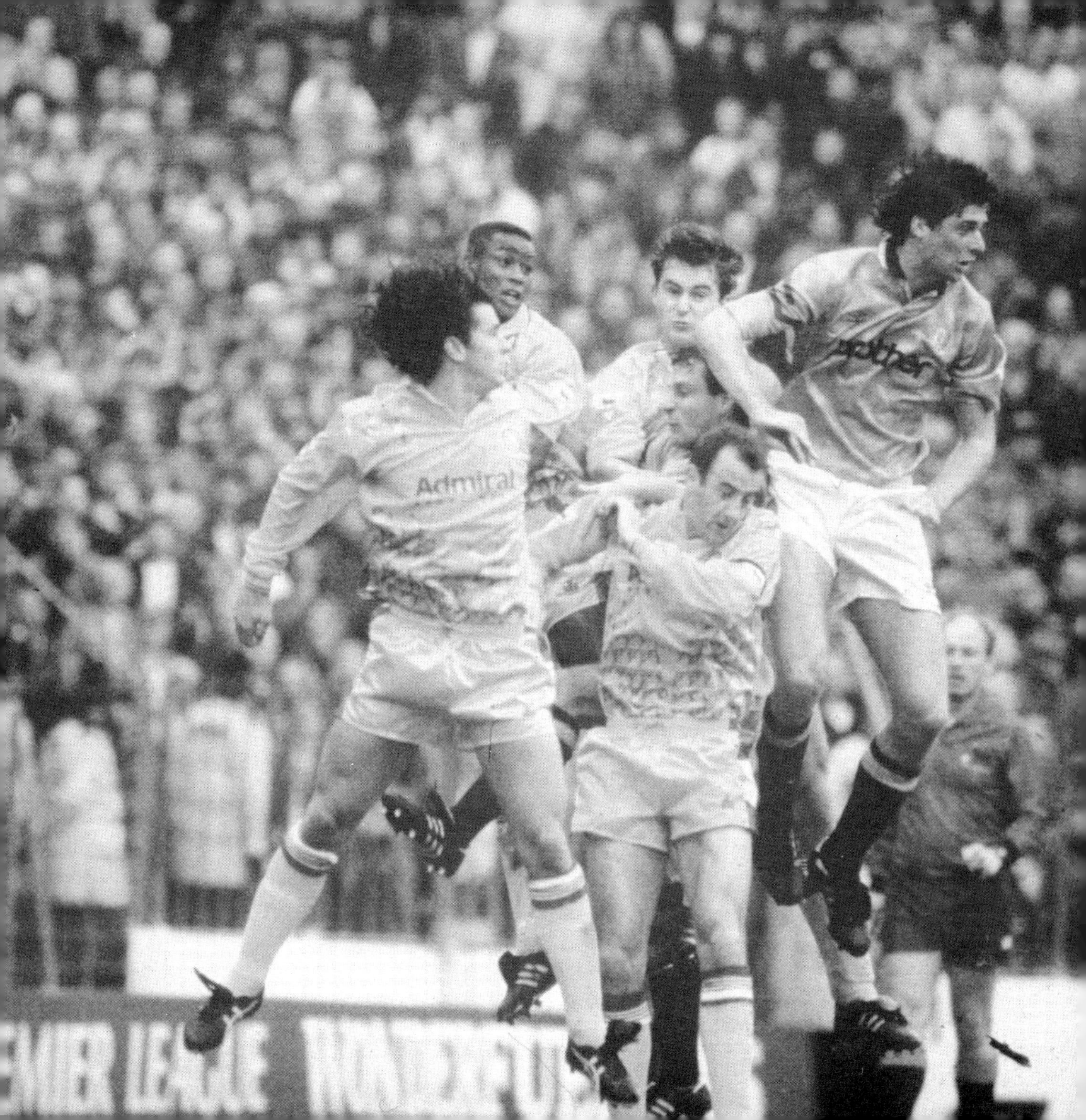
Admiral

games, and then David White made it 2-0 in the 37th minute. A spectacular second half saw City apply even more pressure. The first goals of the season by Andy Hill and Ian Brightwell were in the 75th and 80th minutes. The game ranked as one of the best of the season.

City in Top Six

A confident City faced Coventry at Highfield Road on November 21st, and came out on top with a 3-2 victory despite being tow goals behind early in the second half. Keith Curle scored from a penalty, Rick Holden set up Mike Sheron for his fifth goal in five games, while Niall Quinn provided another for the Blues. Following the Coventry tie, City were sixth in the F.A. Premier League.

November 28th saw the Blues go down 0-1 to Tottenham Hotspur, and this was followed by 1-2, and 1-3 results against Manchester United and Ipswich Town. In this last game, on 12th December, Peter Reid started in the senior side for the first time since September.

Garry Flitcroft scored his first League goal in the Ipswich game, and scored again a week later in the 1-1 draw against Aston Villa on December 19th.

The Christmas period was successful for the Blues who beat Sheffield United 2-0 on December 26th (both goals from David White) and then held Liverpool to a 1-1 draw, with a goal from Niall Quinn, at Anfield two days later.

January 1993

City's first game of 1993 was an F.A. Cup match against Reading, which resulted in a 1-1 draw.

On January 9th, the Blues were away to Chelsea for a Premier League game. Terry Phelan scored his first goal for City in a 4-2 victory. The remaining goals were supplied by White, and Sheron (2).

This was Ray Ranson's first game 'on loan', and David Brightwell was taking part in his second full match of the season.

City entertained Arsenal at Maine Road on January 16th, 1993, three days after beating Reading 4-0 in an F.A. Cup replay game. But despite the fine away results, the Blues could not score against "The Gunners". City had several chances, but the strikers failed to capitalise. The winning Arsenal goal was headed in by Paul Merson.

Boss Peter Reid had problems. Injuries to key players and suspensions reduced the strength of the squad. But, on January 23rd, Michel Vonk made s surprise return in an F.A. Cup match against Queen's Park Rangers. The Dutchman had recovered from his September injury, and supplied one of the goals in the 2-1 victory over Q.P.R.

Michel was in the squad against Oldham Athletic on January 26th when the Blues had a 1-0 victory. A superb cross from Rick Holden was converted into a goal by Niall Quinn's header.

City were now seventh in the F.A. Premier League, while their opponents of January

30th, Blackburn Rovers, were two places higher.

Morale was high in the City camp – with four away wins in a row. The Blues came back from 2-0 down at one stage to being 3-2 on top. City's goals were supplied by Curle (penalty), White and Sheron. This last player's header was his tenth goal in 24 games, while David White's deflected left foot drive gave 'keeper Mimms little chance to pull off a save.

Tony Coton produced some magnificent saves, especially when Jason Wilcox was robbed of a third goal. This was a superb performance by City who turned defeat into a stunning victory.

Leading from the front – Peter Reid tangles with Liverpool's Don Hutchison, watched by Keith Curle, Mike Quigley and Ian Rush

Manchester City

Keith Curle slots home City's second goal from the penalty spot as the Blues fight back from a 0-2 deficit to beat Blackburn Rovers 3-2 in January.

February

In February, City 'keeper Andy Dibble started his fifth loan period during his career at Maine Road. He went to Oldham Athletic on February 2nd because the "Latics" had two senior goalkeepers on the injured list, but instead of representing Oldham against Chelsea, Andy was recalled to Maine Road on 4th February when 'keeper Martyn Margetson hurt his back in training!

The squad travelled to QPR's ground with Andy Dibble acting as substitute goalkeeper. Tony Coton came out for a warm-up before the game but returned to the dressing room feeling unwell. Andy Dibble had to go in nets! He was part of a squad that did well to draw 1-1, particularly since injuries forced McMahon and Quinn to withdraw during the game. City's goal was supplied by Mike Sheron.

The Blues were a respectable 8th in the Premier League on 10th February.

Top of the Premier League, February 10th 1993

TEAM	P	PTS
Manchester United	28	51
Aston Villa	28	50
Norwich City	27	48
Ipswich Town	28	43
Coventry City	28	42
Blackburn Rovers	27	41
QPR	27	41
Manchester City	27	40

Injury Problems

City overcome Barnsley at Maine Road in the Fifth Round of the F.A. Cup, thanks to two goals from David White but then the Blues lost 1-3 to Norwich City on February 20th. Illness kept Peter Reid out of the squad, while Fitzroy Simpson was unable to play because of his suspension. Terry Phelan's damaged hamstring forced him to limp off just before half-time and he was replaced by Andy Hill.

There was a 1-2 defeat at the hands of Sheffield Wednesday, and the Yorkshire club stretched their impressive record to 13 wins in 15 unbeaten games.

Plagued by injury problems, Peter Reid was hoping that Rick Holden and Terry Phelan would be in shape for the clash with Nottingham Forest on February 27th. City won 2-0. White's superb finishing and Flitcroft's delightful skills secured goals in the 19th and 88th minutes.

The players reorganised themselves efficiently as Andy Hill switched to the central defensive position in the absence of skipper Keith Curle who was suffering with a back problem.

The New Stand Opens

March 7th 1993 was an eventful day for City. The ground was surrounded by fans for the first time in the season as the new Umbro stand opened to accommodate an extra 6,500 spectators. This took the capacity to 39,800 and added considerably to the atmosphere.

That Sunday in March was also when City faced Spurs in the F.A. Cup Quarter final. The Blues went down 2-4 to Tottenham, and the game was marred by some mindless spectators who decided to leave their seats and rush onto the pitch.

On Wednesday, March 10th, just over 20,000 people attended the Premier League game with Coventry City, with a 1-0 result. Peter Reid's side had now moved up three places to occupy seventh slot in the Premier League. When City faced Leeds United at Elland Road on Saturday, 13th March, Mike Sheron was replaced by Ray Ranson in the squad. The score was Leeds United 1; Manchester City 0. Peter Reid substituted Sheron for Niall Quinn in the 68th minute. He produced an 18 yard drive eight minutes later, but Lukic kept it out with a magnificent one-handed save.

City-v-United

Just over 37,000 United and City fans packed into Maine Road on March 20th to witness on 11 o'clock kick off for the 118th "derby" game. The 1-1 result was the 44th time the two Manchester giants had drawn in League games.

An inspired cross from Rick Holden in the 57th minute found Niall Quinn, who headed in a magnificent opening goal. The Reds equalised in the 68th minute of this dramatic match. A well-placed cross from Lee Sharpe gave Eric Cantona the chance to score his seventh League goal of the season, as the Frenchman's clever header evaded Tony Coton. This gave United fans with a good reason to cheer and the final result of 1-1 was a fair outcome.

The Spurs Jinx

Spurs were a jinx team for the Blues in 1992/93. The North Londoners had beaten the Maine Road club 4-2 in the Quarter finals of the F.A. Cup. Tottenham also handed out a League defeat earlier in the season and ended Peter Reid's progress in the Coca Cola competition.

On March 24th, City lost 3-1 against a ruthless Spurs squad. The score would have been higher for the London side if it had not been for Tony Coton's tireless efforts to produce some spectacular saves.

Mike Sheron's stylish 60th minute goal was his 14th of the season, and made it 2-1, but the Blues could not manage any more goals against Terry Venables' side.

City in Top Five

The pace and efficiency of Quinn and Reid had a lot to do with City's 3-1 win over Ipswich on Saturday, April 3rd. The Irish international and the player-manager were at the forefront of a slick victory which put the Blues fifth in the Premier League.

Fresh from his impressive goal scoring success in the midweek game for the Republic of Ireland, Niall Quinn led a transformed Manchester City in the second half of the Ipswich game.

Top Of The Premier League, April 4th 1993

TEAM	P	Pts
Norwich	36	65
Aston Villa	35	64
Manchester United	35	63
Blackburn	34	53
Manchester City	35	50
Sheffield Wednesday	33	50

Easter '93

Good Friday at Bramall Lane was the venue for an important clash with Sheffield United. Despite a laboured performance against City, Sheffield United took a vital point from a game resulting in a 1-1 draw. This lifted Sheffield United above Crystal Palace on goal difference at the foot of the Premier League table.

City and Liverpool provided some tremendous Bank Holiday entertainment on Monday, April 12th in spite of City losing White and Sheron towards the end of the first half. Garry Flitcroft gave the Blues an early lead while Vonk, Curle and Phelan kept a Liverpool attack under wraps for most of the first half. The Merseyside equaliser came in the 66th minute, courtesy of Ian Rush, and although this lifted the visitors, Liverpool were unable to score again.

Olden Makes his Mark

The absence of Mike Sheron in the game at Villa Park forced Peter Reid to change his attacking system on April 18th. The Blues were the better side in the first half, taking the lead through a superb header from Niall Quinn, but Villa hit back after the interval to score three times.

It was a crucial victory for Ron Atkinson's team that kept them within a point of Premier League leaders, Manchester United.

City faced Wimbledon at Maine Road on April 21st, having beaten the Selhurst Park club 1-0 in September. Blues had only played Wimbledon eleven times prior to the April '93 encounter.

With Wimbledon being relative newcomers to senior soccer, the teams had met on only eleven previous occasions the Maine Road club had won 3, drawn 6 and lost 2 of these Premier League and Football League matches. A late equaliser from Rick Holden gave City a 1-1 draw.

City set off to Japan after the Wimbledon fixture. A new League was being launched there and City went to help promote the new venture.

On April 27th, the England Under-21 squad had a 3-0 victory over Holland. Mike Sheron supplied two of the goals and set up the third for Spurs' Darren Anderton. The England squad also included City star Garry Flitcroft who again gave a very good account of himself in the national team.

The end of April '93 saw City announce an extension to their agreement with the Brother electronics firm. The sponsorship deal could bring about £2m to Maine Road over the next 3 years, making a nine-year partnership.

May 1993

City travelled to The Dell on May 1st with Steve McMahon back in the side for the first time since a groin injury in February. In this match against Southampton, a confident City dominated the first half. Southampton made more of an effort in the second half but could not dent a formidable Manchester side, and the score remained 0-1 in City's favour, with David White the goalscorer.

When Crystal Palace travelled to Maine Road on May 5th, a 0-0 draw gave them a precious point; after a bland first half, some promising swoops on the Palace defence reminded us of City's forcefulness. In particular, a Quinn effort forced Nigel Martyn to pull off a brilliant one-handed save.

City's last game of the 1992/93 season saw them go down 2-5 to Everton at Maine Road on May 8th, and the Blues finished ninth in the Premier League. Consolation came in the form of a David White header in the 39th minute, his 19th goal of the season, while Curle put away a penalty. The squad for that last 1992/93 Premier League game was:

Margetson; Ranson; Vonk; Curle; Phelan; McMahon; Flitcroft; White; Sheron; Quinn; Holden.

Substitutes: Dibble; Simpson; Kerr.

Things were not easy in 1992/93. Injuries played a major part in the Blues' performance; Steve McMahon, Paul Lake, Michel Vonk, Ian Brightwell and Andy Hill were all plagued by injuries that kept them out of action for several weeks or months.

1992/93 Cup Competitions

The Coca Cola Cup 1992/93

The Coca Cola Cup is a knock-out competition organised by the Football League. It was first introduced as the Football League Cup in 1960. Formerly the Rumbelows League Cup, the competition relies heavily on sponsorship, the current sponsors being Coca Cola.

Second Round, First Leg – September 23rd
City 0, Bristol Rovers 0

Just under 10,000 people watched the West Country club keep a clean sheet. Having completed a three match suspension, Niall Quinn returned in this first Cup tie of the season.

Second Round, Second Leg – October 7th
Bristol Rovers 1 Manchester City 2

City travelled to Twerton Park and produced a 2-1 victory. The closing minutes of the game in extra time saw the Blues snatch the winner and although credited to Niall Quinn, the first goal was deflected off a Bristol Rovers' player. Rick Holden scored the vital winning goal.

Third Round – October 28th
Manchester City 0, Tottenham Hotspur 1

City and Tottenham had never met in the League Cup, but there have been 9 ties between the clubs in the FA Cup. The last

Moments to Remember

tie between the two clubs at Maine Road was in 1969, when Francis Lee's goal gave them victory. The 1992 meeting of the clubs culminated in a 0-1 win for the Londoners, when a Vinny Samways goal allowed Tottenham to face Nottingham Forest in the next round.

The F.A. Cup 1992/93

F.A. Cup Third Round – January 2nd
Manchester City 1 Reading 1

Second Division Reading went ahead in the 45th minute with a Taylor goal, but pressure by the Blues in the second half resulted in Mike Sheron seizing an equaliser, from a Garry Flitcroft through-ball.

F.A. Cup Third Round – January 13th
Reading 0 Manchester City 4

This was an exciting replay, a Mike Sheron goal in the 3rd minute of the game proving to be a tremendous fillip for City. Rick Holden netted one half an hour later, while Garry Flitcroft and Niall Quinn scored in the 69th and 72nd minute.

F.A. Cup Fourth Round – January 23rd
Q.P.R. 1 Manchester City 2

David White and Michel Vonk supplied the two goals for City's victory here, the Dutchman making his full Cup debut for the Blues. Interestingly, this made City the first visiting team to win at Q.P.R. in the F.A. Cup since 1980.

F.A. Cup Fifth Round – February 13th
Manchester City 2 Barnsley 0

Barnsley boss Mel Machin, former City manager, saw his old club produce a 2-0 defeat, David White scoring both goals.

An excellent save by Tony Coton prevented the Yorkshire side from scoring in the first half. In the second half of the game, Coton continued to pull off good saves from efforts by Currie and Rammell.

F.A. Cup Sixth Round – March 7th
Manchester City 2 Tottenham Hotspur 4

There was a joyous mood at Maine Road for this game, as the impressive Umbro Stand was used for the first time after a construction programme lasting 11 months.

Sadly, a 2-4 result meant that the Blues would not go on to the Semi-finals of the F.A. Cup. However, both sides played well, their enterprising soccer serving to compensate for the actions of some mindless elements in the crowd, who at one stage ran onto the pitch.

More to look forward to!

Young players like Sheron and Flitcroft made huge strides for both club and country while the team's high point was undoubtedly

The Maine Road side provided some entertaining soccer in the F.A. Cup when they reached the sixth round. City are a major force in English soccer and the recent strengthening of the senior squad will no doubt bring even more enjoyment for the fans in the 1993/4 season.

Manchester City

City's Games - 1992/93

Date	Opponents	Result	Scorers
August 1992			
17	Queen's Park Rangers	1-1	White
19	Middlesborough	0-2	
22	Blackburn Rovers	0-1	
26	Norwich City	3-1	White (2) McMahon
29	Oldham Athletic	3-3	Quinn, Vonk, White
September 1992			
1	Wimbledon	1-0	White
5	Sheffield Wednesday	3-0	White (2), Vonk
12	Middlesborough	0-1	
20	Chelsea	0-1	
23	Bristol Rovers (CCC 2/1)	0-0	
28	Arsenal	0-1	
October 1992			
3	Nottingham Forest	2-2	Holden, Simpson
7	Bristol Rovers (CCC 2/2)	2-1	Quinn, Holden
17	Crystal Palace	0-0	
24	Southampton	1-0	Sheron
28	Tottenham Hotspur (CCC 3)	0-1	
31	Everton	3-1	Sheron (2), White
November 1992			
7	Leeds United	4-0	Sheron, White, Hill, Brightwell
21	Coventry City	3-2	Sheron, Quinn, Curle (pen)
28	Tottenham Hotspur	0-1	
December 1992			
6	Manchester United	1-2	Quinn
12	Ipswich Town	1-3	Flitcroft
19	Aston Villa	1-1	Flitcroft
26	Sheffield United	2-0	White (2)
28	Liverpool	1-1	Quinn
January 1993			
2	Reading (FAC 3)	1-1	Sheron
9	Chelsea	4-2	White, Sheron (2), Phelan
13	Reading (FAC 3 replay)	4-0	Sheron, Holden, Flitcroft, Quinn
16	Arsenal	0-1	
23	Queen's Park Rangers (FAC 4)	2-1	White, Vonk
26	Oldham Athletic	1-0	Quinn
30	Blackburn Rovers	3-2	Sheron, Curle (pen), White
February 1993			
6	Queen's Park Rangers	1-1	Sheron
13	Barnsley (FAC 5)	2-0	White (2)
20	Norwich City	1-2	Sheron
23	Sheffield Wednesday	1-2	Quinn
27	Nottingham Forest	2-0	White, Flitcroft
March 1993			
7	Tottenham (FAC 6)	2-4	Sheron, Phelan
10	Coventry City	1-0	Flitcroft
13	Leeds United	0-1	
20	Manchester United	1-1	Quinn
24	Tottenham Hotspur	1-3	Sheron
April 1993			
3	Ipswich Town	3-1	Quinn, Holden, Vonk
9	Sheffield United	1-1	Own goal
12	Liverpool	1-1	Flitcroft
18	Aston Villa	1-3	Quinn
21	Wimbledon	1-1	Holden
May 1993			
1	Southampton	1-0	White
5	Crystal Palace	0-0	
8	Everton	2-5	White, Curle (pen)

CCC – Coca Cola Cup
FAC – F.A. Cup

Honours gained by Manchester City

Football League
Division One Champions: (2)
1936-37, 1967-68
Runners-up (3)
1903-04, 1920-21, 1976-77
Division Two Champions: (6)
1898-99, 1902-03, 1927-28, 1946-47, 1965-66
Runners-up (3)
1895-96, 1950-51, 1988-89

FA Cup
Winners: (4)
1904, 1934, 1956, 1969
Runners-up (4)
1926, 1933, 1955, 1981

Football League Cup
Winners: (2)
1970, 1976
Runners-up: 1973-74

European Competition
European Cup: 1968-69
European Cup Winners' Cup:
1969-70 (Winners), 1970-71
UEFA Cup: 1972-73, 1976-77, 1977-78
1978-79

Full Members' Cup
Runners-up: 1986

FA Youth Cup
Winners: 1986

Central League
Champions: 1977-78, 1986-87

FA Charity Shield
Winners: (3) 1937, 1968, 1972

More books to remember . . . from Sigma Leisure

We publish a wide range of general interest books, including:

THE INCREDIBLY BIASED BEER GUIDE: a celebration of Britain's small breweries. (£6.95)

I REMAIN –YOUR SON JACK, a collection of letters from the first World. (£8.95)

PEAK DISTRICT DIARY – a superbly illustrated collection of Roger Redfern's best articles in *The Guardian* newspaper. (£7.95)

DIAL 999 – EMERGENCY SERVICES IN ACTION: an illustrated collection of archive and current material. (£9.95)

Local History:

PORTRAIT OF MACCLESFIELD

PORTRAIT OF MANCHESTER

PORTRAIT OF STOCKPORT

PORTRAIT OF WARRINGTON

REFLECTIONS ON BLACKPOOL

REFLECTIONS ON LANCASTER

REFLECTIONS ON PRESTON

OLD NOTTINGHAMSHIRE REMEMBERED

(All £6.95)

Pub Walks Books

Sample the delights of country pubs all over England, and enjoy some of the finest walks with our expanding range of 'real ale' books:

- PUB WALKS IN THE PEAK DISTRICT
  - Les Lumsdon and Martin Smith
- MORE PUB WALKS IN THE PEAK DISTRICT – Les Lumsdon and Martin Smith
- PUB WALKS IN LANCASHIRE – Neil Coates
- PUB WALKS IN THE PENNINES
  – Les Lumsdon and Colin Speakman
- PUB WALKS IN THE LAKE DISTRICT – Neil Coates
- PUB WALKS IN THE YORKSHIRE DALES – Clive Price
- PUB WALKS IN THE COTSWOLDS – Laurence Main
- HEREFORDSHIRE WALKS – REAL ALE AND CIDER COUNTRY – Les Lumsdon
- PUB WALKS IN CHESHIRE – Jen Darling

- all 'Pub Walks' books are just £6.95 each

Even more books from Sigma Leisure . . .

There are even more books for outdoor people in our catalogue, including:

- EAST CHESHIRE WALKS – Graham Beech
- WEST CHESHIRE WALKS – Jen Darling
- WEST PENNINE WALKS – Mike Cresswell
- NEWARK AND SHERWOOD RAMBLES – Malcolm McKenzie
- RAMBLES AROUND MANCHESTER – Mike Cresswell
- WESTERN LAKELAND RAMBLES – Gordon Brown
- WELSH WALKS: Dolgellau and the Cambrian Coast – Laurence Main and Morag Perrott
- WELSH WALKS: Aberystwyth and District – Laurence Main and Morag Perrott
- OFF-BEAT CYCLING IN THE PEAK DISTRICT – Clive Smith
- THE GREATER MANCHESTER BOUNDARY WALK – Graham Phythian
- THE THIRLMERE WAY – Tim Cappelli
- THE MARCHES WAY – Les Lumsdon

We also publish:

- Guidebooks for local towns
- A guide to the 'Pubs of Old Lancashire'
- Spooky stories
- Myths and Legends

Under our Sigma Press banner, we publish over 100 computer books including **The PC Games Bible** – the only definitive guide to the gaming scene.

All of our books are available from your local bookshop.

In case of difficulty, or to obtain our complete catalogue, please contact:

**Sigma Leisure,
1 South Oak Lane,
Wilmslow, Cheshire SK9 6AR
Phone: 0625 – 531035 Fax: 0625 – 536800**

ACCESS and VISA orders welcome – call our friendly sales staff or use our 24 hour Answerphone service!

Most orders are despatched on the day we receive your order – you could be enjoying our books in just a couple of days.